NFPA® 31

Standard for the

Installation of Oil-Burning Equipment

2011 Edition

This edition of NFPA 31, *Standard for the Installation of Oil-Burning Equipment*, was prepared by the Technical Committee on Liquid Fuel Burning Equipment. It was issued by the Standards Council on December 14, 2010, with an effective date of January 3, 2011, and supersedes all previous editions.

This edition of NFPA 31 was approved as an American National Standard on January 3, 2011.

Origin and Development of NFPA 31

Oil-burning equipment standards date from 1902, when they were issued by the National Board of Fire Underwriters under the title *Rules and Requirements of the National Board of Fire Underwriters for the Storage and Use of Fuel Oil and for the Construction and Installation of Oil Burning Equipments.* Subsequently, the project was turned over to the NFPA and a completely revised standard was first presented to the Association in 1913. Since then, the responsibility for NFPA 31 has been that of the Technical Committee on Liquid Fuel Burning Equipment. Revised editions of NFPA 31 were issued in 1948, 1951, 1953, 1955, 1956, 1957, 1959, 1961, 1963, 1964, 1965, 1968, 1972, 1974, 1978, 1983, 1987, 1992, 1997, 2001, 2006, and 2010.

The 1997 edition of NFPA 31 (processed through the November 1996 document revision cycle) incorporated the following major amendments to the previous edition:

(1) Editorial revision of Chapter 1, General, to effect editorial improvement and to comply with the *Manual of Style for NFPA Technical Committee Documents*
(2) Numerous amendments to the definitions to eliminate inconsistencies with NFPA 97, *Standard Glossary of Terms Relating to Chimneys, Vents, and Heat-Producing Appliances*
(3) Numerous amendments to the requirements for chimneys and chimney connectors in Section 1.11, formerly Section 1.7
(4) New requirements for termination of flue gas venting systems in 1.12.3, Termination of Venting Systems
(5) A complete revision of Chapter 2, Tank Storage
(6) A new version of Table 4.4.1.1, Clearances to Combustible Materials
(7) A complete revision of Chapter 5, Installation of Heating and Cooking Appliances
(8) A new Appendix D, Considerations for Combustion Equipment Firing Alternative (Non-petroleum) Fuels
(9) A new Appendix E, Relining Masonry Chimneys, to provide needed guidance for evaluation, repair, and relining of existing masonry chimneys when replacing heating systems with high efficiency combustion appliances

The 2001 edition of NFPA 31 (processed through the November 2000 document revision cycle) included the following major changes:

(1) A major editorial reorganization of the text to comply with a new edition of the *Manual of Style for NFPA Technical Committee Documents*
(2) Recognition of nonmetallic fuel oil storage tanks for inside use
(3) A return to the 1¼ in. (32 mm) vent diameter for inside fuel oil storage tanks, based on full-scale fire tests
(4) An increase in the number of storage tanks that can be manifolded together, if the tanks are part of an engineered fuel storage system
(5) Appendix text to 10.5.4 (4-3.4 in the 1997 edition) that provides guidance on the appropriate types of limit controls for the various appliances
(6) A new Chapter 12 to address appliances that can burn used oil
(7) A new Chapter 13 to address appliances that can burn either gaseous fuels or fuel oil
(8) Major revisions to Appendix E, Relining Masonry Chimneys

The 2006 edition of NFPA 31 (processed through the November 2005 document revision cycle) incorporated the following major amendments:

(1) Revised guidance in 6.6.7 for inspecting the chimney or flue gas venting system prior to installation of oil-fired appliances. The guidance limits the scope of this inspection, but requires written notification of deficiencies to the owner of the premises.
(2) Updated design standards and installation requirements for fuel oil storage tanks.
(3) Complete revision of Section 7.5 on installation of fuel oil storage tanks in buildings. Included is replacement of previous criteria for allowable storage quantities in unenclosed and enclosed environments with the simpler criteria used by NFPA 37, *Standard for the Installation and Use of Stationary Combustion Engines and Gas Turbines*. Also included is guidance for manifolding of three- and four-tank systems.
(4) More specific guidance in Section 7.5 for installation of oil safety valves and thermally operated shutoff valves.
(5) Stricter requirements for taking fuel storage systems out of service, either temporarily or permanently.
(6) More specific requirements in Section 8.9 for testing piping installations.

The 2011 edition of NFPA 31 (processed through the November 2010 document revision cycle) incorporates the following major amendments:

(1) Amendments to Scope and Purpose statements to allow the use of any liquid fuel deemed appropriate for use for stationary liquid fuel burning appliances, including fuels derived from biodiesel sources
(2) Replacement of the definition of *fuel oil* with one for *liquid fuel*, to include biodiesel fuel blend stocks
(3) Expansion of the types of fuels deemed acceptable for use within the scope of NFPA 31 and recognition of the appropriate specifications
(4) Amendments to Section 6.5 to clarify the provisions for installation of chimney connectors to chimney lining systems; to allow the use of listed factory-built chimney connectors; and to establish the minimum thickness for steel pipe chimney connectors
(5) Addition of a requirement to verify proper size of the chimney or flue gas venting system when a new or replacement appliance is installed
(6) Complete revision of Chapter 7, Liquid Fuel Tanks, to clarify the requirements for proper installation of storage tanks and to recognize all liquid fuels acceptable for use within the scope of NFPA 31
(7) Relocation of certain piping-related provisions from Chapter 7 to Chapter 8, where they more properly belong
(8) Complete revision of Chapter 8, Heating Fuel Piping Systems and Components, to clarify the requirements for proper installation of piping systems and to recognize all liquid fuels acceptable for use within the scope of NFPA 31
(9) Amendment to 10.6.1 and Table 10.6.1 to allow spacing between appliances of a multi-unit installation in accordance with manufacturer's instructions

Technical Committee on Liquid Fuel Burning Equipment

Allen L. Pirro, *Chair*
Intertek Testing Services, NY [RT]

Edward Angelone, National Grid, NY [U]
John E. Batey, Energy Research Center, Inc., CT [M]
Rep. Oilheat Manufacturers Association
Robert V. Boltz, Vincent R. Boltz, Inc., PA [IM]
Rep. National Association of Oil Heating Service Managers, Inc.
Aaron J. Clark, Lipton Energy Inc., MA [IM]
Brian C. Donovan, STICO Mutual Insurance Company, IL [I]
Jack Frederick, Frederick Geraghty Incorporated, MA [M]
David P. Horowitz, Tighe & Bond, MA [SE]
John J. Huber, National Oilheat Research Alliance, VA [C]
Marek Kulik, Technical Standards and Safety Authority, Canada [E]
George M. Kusterer, Bock Water Heaters, PA [M]
Yves Legault, Granby Industries, Canada [M]
John D. Maniscalco, New York Oil Heating Association, NY [IM]

Michael S. Markarian, New England Institute of Technology, RI [SE]
Jay McCay, Farm & Home Oil Company, PA [IM]
Paul W. Moody, State of Maine, ME [E]
Edward J. Peznowski, Connecticut Department of Public Safety, CT [E]
John J. Pilger, Chief Chimney Services, Inc., NY [IM]
Rep. National Chimney Sweep Guild
Roland A. Riegel, Underwriters Laboratories Inc., NY [RT]
Earl J. Rightmier, AERCO International, Inc., NJ [M]
Rep. Air-Conditioning, Heating, & Refrigeration Institute
David C. Schildwachter Sr., Fred M. Schildwachter & Sons, Inc., NY [IM]
Rep. Petroleum Marketers Association of America
Bernard A. Smith, Concord Energy Options, MA [SE]
Charles R. Tibboles, R. W. Beckett Corporation, OH [M]

Alternates

Travis F. Hardin, Underwriters Laboratories Inc., NC [RT]
(Alt. to R. A. Riegel)
Robert G. Hedden, Oilheat Associates, VT [M]
(Alt. to J. E. Batey)

Dale D. Hersey, State of Maine, ME [E]
(Alt. to P. W. Moody)
John F. Levey, Oilheat Associates, Inc., NY [C]
(Alt. to J. J. Huber)

Robert P. Benedetti, NFPA Staff Liaison

This list represents the membership at the time the Committee was balloted on the final text of this edition. Since that time, changes in the membership may have occurred. A key to classifications is found at the back of the document.

NOTE: Membership on a committee shall not in and of itself constitute an endorsement of the Association or any document developed by the committee on which the member serves.

Committee Scope: This Committee shall have primary responsibility for documents on the safeguarding against the fire, explosion, and life safety hazards associated with the installation and use of stationary and portable liquid fuel-burning equipment, including: (1) related fuel storage tanks and associated piping, venting systems, pumps, and controls; (2) the combustion air supply and flue gas venting systems for the liquid fuel burning equipment; and (3) combustion and safety controls. This Committee does not have have responsibility for: (1) boiler-furnaces with fuel input ratings of 3660 kW (12,500,000 BTU per hr. or 10,000 lbs. steam per hr.) or more; (2) process ovens; (3) process furnaces; or (4) internal combustion engines.

Contents

NFPA 31

Standard for the

Installation of Oil-Burning Equipment

2011 Edition

IMPORTANT NOTE: This NFPA document is made available for use subject to important notices and legal disclaimers. These notices and disclaimers appear in all publications containing this document and may be found under the heading "Important Notices and Disclaimers Concerning NFPA Documents." They can also be obtained on request from NFPA or viewed at www.nfpa.org/disclaimers.

NOTICE: An asterisk (*) following the number or letter designating a paragraph indicates that explanatory material on the paragraph can be found in Annex A.

Changes other than editorial are indicated by a vertical rule beside the paragraph, table, or figure in which the change occurred. These rules are included as an aid to the user in identifying changes from the previous edition. Where one or more complete paragraphs have been deleted, the deletion is indicated by a bullet (•) between the paragraphs that remain.

A reference in brackets [ ] following a section or paragraph indicates material that has been extracted from another NFPA document. As an aid to the user, the complete title and edition of the source documents for extracts in mandatory sections of the document are given in Chapter 2 and those for extracts in informational sections are given in Annex F. Extracted text may be edited for consistency and style and may include the revision of internal paragraph references and other references as appropriate. Requests for interpretations or revisions of extracted text shall be sent to the technical committee responsible for the source document.

Information on referenced publications can be found in Chapter 2 and Annex F.

Chapter 1   Administration

1.1 Scope.

1.1.1 This standard shall apply to the installation of stationary liquid fuel–burning appliances, including but not limited to industrial-, commercial-, and residential-type steam, hot water, or warm air heating appliances; domestic-type range burners; space heaters; and portable liquid fuel–burning equipment.

1.1.2 This standard shall also apply to all accessories and control systems, whether electric, thermostatic, or mechanical, and all electrical wiring connected to liquid fuel–burning appliances.

1.1.3 This standard shall also apply to the installation of liquid fuel storage and supply systems connected to liquid fuel–burning appliances.

1.1.4 This standard shall also apply to those multifueled appliances in which a liquid fuel is one of the standard or optional fuels.

1.1.5* This standard shall not apply to internal combustion engines, oil lamps, or portable devices not specifically covered in this standard. *(See Chapter 11 for portable devices that are covered in this standard.)*

1.2 Purpose. The purpose of this standard is to provide minimum requirements for the safe installation of stationary liquid fuel–burning appliances and all related accessories so as to prevent fires and explosions.

1.3 Application. (Reserved)

1.4 Retroactivity. The provisions of this standard reflect a consensus of what is necessary to provide an acceptable degree of protection from the hazards addressed in this standard at the time the standard was issued.

1.4.1 Unless otherwise specified, the provisions of this standard shall not apply to facilities, equipment, structures, or installations that existed or were approved for construction or installation prior to the effective date of the standard. Where specified, the provisions of this standard shall be retroactive.

1.4.2 In those cases where the authority having jurisdiction determines that the existing situation presents an unacceptable degree of risk, the authority having jurisdiction shall be permitted to apply retroactively any portions of this standard deemed appropriate.

1.4.3 The retroactive requirements of this standard shall be permitted to be modified if their application clearly would be impractical in the judgment of the authority having jurisdiction, and only where it is clearly evident that a reasonable degree of safety is provided.

1.5 Equivalency. Nothing in this standard is intended to prevent the use of systems, methods, or devices of equivalent or superior quality, strength, fire resistance, effectiveness, durability, and safety over those prescribed by this standard.

1.5.1 Technical documentation shall be submitted to the authority having jurisdiction to demonstrate equivalency.

1.5.2 The system, method, or device shall be approved for the intended purpose by the authority having jurisdiction.

1.6 Units.

1.6.1 The units of measure in this standard are presented first in U.S. customary units (inch/pound units). International System (SI) of Units follow the inch/pound units in parentheses.

1.6.2 Either system of units shall be acceptable for satisfying the requirements in the standard.

1.6.3 Users of this standard shall apply one system of units consistently and shall not alternate between units.

1.6.4 The values presented for measurements in this standard are expressed with a degree of precision appropriate for practical application and enforcement. It is not intended that the application or enforcement of these values be more precise than the precision expressed.

1.6.5 Where extracted text contains values expressed in only one system of units, the values in the extracted text have been retained without conversion to preserve the values established by the responsible technical committee in the source documents.

1.7 Code Adoption Requirements. (Reserved)

Chapter 2   Referenced Publications

2.1 General. The documents or portions thereof listed in this chapter are referenced within this standard and shall be considered part of the requirements of this document.

2.2 NFPA Publications. National Fire Protection Association, 1 Batterymarch Park, Quincy, MA 02169-7471.

NFPA 13, *Standard for the Installation of Sprinkler Systems*, 2010 edition.

NFPA 15, *Standard for Water Spray Fixed Systems for Fire Protection*, 2007 edition.

NFPA 30, *Flammable and Combustible Liquids Code*, 2008 edition.

NFPA 30A, *Code for Motor Fuel Dispensing Facilities and Repair Garages*, 2008 edition.

NFPA 54, *National Fuel Gas Code*, 2009 edition.

NFPA 70®, National Electrical Code®, 2011 edition.

NFPA 80, *Standard for Fire Doors and Other Opening Protectives*, 2010 edition.

NFPA 85, *Boiler and Combustion Systems Hazards Code*, 2011 edition.

NFPA 86, *Standard for Ovens and Furnaces*, 2011 edition.

NFPA 90A, *Standard for the Installation of Air-Conditioning and Ventilating Systems*, 2009 edition.

NFPA 90B, *Standard for the Installation of Warm Air Heating and Air-Conditioning Systems*, 2009 edition.

NFPA 211, *Standard for Chimneys, Fireplaces, Vents, and Solid Fuel–Burning Appliances*, 2010 edition.

2.3 Other Publications.

2.3.1 API Publications.   American Petroleum Institute, 1220 L Street, NW, Washington, DC 20005-4070.

API Standard 650, *Welded Steel Tanks for Oil Storage*, 11th edition, 2007.

2.3.2 ASME Publications.   American Society of Mechanical Engineers, Three Park Avenue, New York, NY 10016-5990.

ANSI/ASME B36.10M, *Standard on Welded and Seamless Wrought Steel Pipe*, 2004.

Boiler and Pressure Vessel Code, 2007.

2.3.3 ASTM Publications.   ASTM International, 100 Barr Harbor Drive, P.O. Box C700, West Conshohocken, PA 19428-2959.

ASTM A 53/53M, *Welded and Seamless Steel Pipe (Black & Galvanized)*, 2010.

ASTM A 106, *Seamless Carbon Steel Pipe (High Temp Service)*, 2010.

ASTM A 254, *Copper-Brazed Steel Tubing*, 1997 (2007).

ASTM A 269, *Seamless & Welded Stainless Steel Tubing*, 2010.

ASTM B 43, *Seamless Red Brass Pipe*, 2009.

ASTM B 75, *Seamless Copper Tube*, 2002.

ASTM B 88, *Seamless Copper Water Tube*, 2009.

ASTM B 135, *Seamless Brass Tube*, 2010.

ASTM B 280, *Seamless Copper Tube for Air Conditioning & Refrigeration Service*, 2008.

ASTM D 396, *Standard Specification for Fuel Oils*, 2010.

ASTM D 3699, *Standard Specification for Kerosene*, 2008.

ASTM D 6448, *Industrial Burner Fuels from Used Lube Oils*, 2009.

ASTM D 6751, *Standard Specification for Biodiesel Fuel Blend Stock (B100) for Middle Distillate Fuels*, 2010.

ASTM D 6823, *Commercial Burner Fuels from Used Lube Oils*, 2008.

2.3.4 CAN/CGSB Publications.   Canadian General Standards Board, Place du Portage III, 6B1, 11 Laurier Street, Gatineau, QC, K1A 1G6, Canada.

CAN/CGSB 3.2-99(2), *Heating Fuel Oil*, 2007.

2.3.5 UL Publications.   Underwriters Laboratories Inc., 333 Pfingsten Road, Northbrook, IL 60062-2096.

UL 30, *Metal Safety Cans*, 1995.

UL 58, *Standard for Steel Underground Tanks for Flammable and Combustible Liquids*, 1996.

ANSI/UL 80, *Standard for Steel Tanks for Oil-Burner Fuels and Other Combustible Liquids*, 2007.

ANSI/UL 103, *Standard for Factory Built Chimneys for Residential Type and Building Heating Appliances*, 2010.

ANSI/UL 142, *Standard for Steel Aboveground Tanks for Flammable and Combustible Liquids*, 2006.

ANSI/UL 296, *Standard for Oil Burners*, 2009.

ANSI/UL 296A, *Standard for Waste Oil-Burning Air-Heating Appliances*, 1995.

ANSI/UL 443, *Standard for Steel Auxiliary Tanks for Oil Burner Fuel*, 2006.

UL 795, *Standard for Commercial Industrial Gas-Heating Equipment*, 2006.

UL 971, *Underground Nonmetallic Piping for Flammable Liquids*, 1995.

UL 1313, *Nonmetallic Safety Cans for Petroleum Products*, 1993.

UL 1316, *Standard for Glass-Fiber-Reinforced Plastic Underground Storage Tanks for Petroleum Products, Alcohols, and Alcohol-Gasoline Mixtures*, 2006.

ANSI/UL 1746, *Standard for External Corrosion Protection Systems for Steel Underground Storage Tanks*, 2007.

UL 2080, *Standard for Fire Resistant Tanks for Flammable and Combustible Liquids*, 2000.

ANSI/UL 2085, *Standard for Protected Aboveground Tanks for Flammable and Combustible Liquids*, 1997.

UL 2245, *Standard for Below-Grade Vaults for Flammable Liquid Storage Tanks*, 2006.

SU 971A, *Underground Metallic Piping for Flammable Liquids*, 2006.

SU 2258, *Outline of Investigation for Nonmetallic Tanks for Oil Burner Fuels and Other Combustible Liquids*, 1999.

2.3.6 U.S. Government Publications.   U.S. Government Printing Office, Washington DC 20402.

Title 40, Code of Federal Regulations, Part 279.23, "On-Site Burning in Space Heaters."

2.3.7 Other Publications. *Merriam-Webster's Collegiate Dictionary,* 11th edition, Merriam-Webster, Inc., Springfield, MA, 2003.

2.4 References for Extracts in Mandatory Sections.

NFPA 54, *National Fuel Gas Code,* 2009 edition.

NFPA 70®, National Electrical Code®, 2011 edition.

NFPA 86, *Standard for Ovens and Furnaces,* 2011 edition.

NFPA 211, *Standard for Chimneys, Fireplaces, Vents, and Solid Fuel–Burning Appliances,* 2010 edition.

NFPA 1451, *Standard for a Fire Service Vehicle Operations Training Program,* 2007 edition.

Chapter 3   Definitions

3.1 General. The definitions contained in this chapter shall apply to the terms used in this standard. Where terms are not defined in this chapter or within another chapter, they shall be defined using their ordinarily accepted meanings within the context in which they are used. *Merriam-Webster's Collegiate Dictionary,* 11th edition, shall be the source for the ordinarily accepted meaning.

3.2 NFPA Official Definitions.

3.2.1* Approved. Acceptable to the authority having jurisdiction.

3.2.2* Authority Having Jurisdiction (AHJ). An organization, office, or individual responsible for enforcing the requirements of a code or standard, or for approving equipment, materials, an installation, or a procedure.

3.2.3 Labeled. Equipment or materials to which has been attached a label, symbol, or other identifying mark of an organization that is acceptable to the authority having jurisdiction and concerned with product evaluation, that maintains periodic inspection of production of labeled equipment or materials, and by whose labeling the manufacturer indicates compliance with appropriate standards or performance in a specified manner.

3.2.4* Listed. Equipment, materials, or services included in a list published by an organization that is acceptable to the authority having jurisdiction and concerned with evaluation of products or services, that maintains periodic inspection of production of listed equipment or materials or periodic evaluation of services, and whose listing states that either the equipment, material, or service meets appropriate designated standards or has been tested and found suitable for a specified purpose.

3.2.5 Shall. Indicates a mandatory requirement.

3.2.6 Should. Indicates a recommendation or that which is advised but not required.

3.2.7 Standard. A document, the main text of which contains only mandatory provisions using the word "shall" to indicate requirements and which is in a form generally suitable for mandatory reference by another standard or code or for adoption into law. Nonmandatory provisions shall be located in an appendix or annex, footnote, or fine-print note and are not to be considered a part of the requirements of a standard.

3.3 General Definitions.

3.3.1 Air Heater. An indirect-fired appliance intended to supply heated air for space heating and other purposes, but not intended for permanent installation.

3.3.2 Antiflooding Device. A safety control that causes the flow of (liquid) fuel to be shut off when a rise in fuel level occurs or when excess fuel is received and that operates before the hazardous discharge of fuel can occur.

3.3.3 Appliance.

3.3.3.1 *Industrial Low-Heat Appliance.* An industrial appliance such as a floor-mounted or suspended-type warm-air furnace that is larger than 100 ft^3 (2.8 m^3) in size, excluding blower compartment, fan compartment, and burner equipment; a steam boiler that operates at pressures that do not exceed a gauge pressure of 50 psi (gauge pressure of 345 kPa) and is larger than 100 ft^3 (2.8 m^3) in size, excluding burner equipment; a water boiler that operates at water temperatures of not more than the temperature of saturated steam at pressures that do not exceed a gauge pressure of 50 psi (gauge pressure of 345 kPa) and is larger than 100 ft^3 (2.8 m^3), excluding burner equipment; a floor mounted or suspended type unit heater larger than 100 ft^3 (2.8 m^3) in size, excluding blower compartment, fan compartment, and burner equipment; a commercial cooking range; a bake oven; a candy furnace; a stereotype furnace; a drying and curing appliance; or any other process appliance in which materials are heated or melted at temperatures (excluding flue gas temperature) that do not exceed 600°F (316°C).

3.3.3.2 *Industrial Medium-Heat Appliance.* A steam boiler that operates at pressures that exceed a gauge pressure of 50 psi (gauge pressure of 345 kPa) or an industrial appliance larger than 100 ft^3 (2.8 m^3) in size, excluding blower compartment, fan compartment, and burner equipment, such as an annealing furnace (glass or metal), a charcoal furnace, a galvanizing furnace, a gas producer, or a commercial or industrial incinerator.

3.3.3.3 *Industrial High-Heat Appliance.* An industrial appliance that is larger than 100 ft^3 (2.8 m^3) in size, excluding blower compartment, fan compartment, and burner equipment, such as a billet or bloom furnace, a blast furnace, a brass melter, a cupola, a glass furnace, an open-hearth furnace, a ceramic kiln, or a vitreous enameling oven for ferrous materials.

3.3.4 Boiler. A closed vessel in which water is heated, steam is generated, steam is superheated, or in which any combination thereof takes place by the application of heat from combustible fuels, in a self-contained or attached furnace.

3.3.4.1 *High Pressure Boiler.* A boiler for generating steam at gauge pressures in excess of 15 psi (gauge pressure of 103 kPa), or for heating water to a temperature in excess of 250°F (121°C) or at a gauge pressure in excess of 160 psi (gauge pressure of 1100 kPa).

3.3.4.2 *Hot Water Supply Boiler.* A low-pressure hot water boiler having a volume exceeding 120 gal (454 L), or a heat input exceeding 200,000 Btu/hr (58.6 kW), or an operating temperature exceeding 200°F (93°C) that provides hot water to be used outside the boiler.

3.3.4.3 *Low Pressure Boiler.* A boiler for generating steam at gauge pressures not in excess of 15 psi (gauge pressure of 103 kPa) or for furnishing water at a maximum temperature of 250°F (121°C) at a maximum gauge pressure of 160 psi (gauge pressure of 1100 kPa).

3.3.5 Btu. Abbreviation for British thermal unit. The quantity of heat needed to raise the temperature of 1 pound of water 1°F.

3.3.6 Burner.

3.3.6.1 *Automatically Ignited Burner.* A burner equipped so that the main burner fuel can be turned on and ignited automatically.

3.3.6.2 *Manually Ignited Burner.* A burner equipped so that the main burner fuel is turned on only by hand and ignited under supervision.

3.3.6.3 *Mechanical Draft–Type Burner.* A burner that includes a power-driven fan, blower, or other mechanism as the primary means for supplying the air for combustion.

3.3.6.4 *Natural Draft–Type Burner.* A burner that depends primarily on the natural draft created in the chimney or venting system to induce the air required for combustion into the burner.

3.3.7* **Central Heating Appliance.** A stationary heating appliance comprising the following: boilers, central furnaces, floor furnaces, and wall furnaces.

3.3.8 **Centralized Oil Distribution System.** A system of piping through which oil is supplied from a remote central supply tank or tanks to one or more buildings, mobile homes, recreational vehicles, or other structures.

3.3.9 **Chimney.** A structure containing one or more vertical or nearly vertical passageways for conveying flue gases to the outside atmosphere. [**211**, 2010]

3.3.9.1 *Factory-Built Chimney.*

3.3.9.1.1 *Building Heating Appliance–Type Factory-Built Chimney.* A heating appliance chimney suitable for continuous use at 1000°F (538°C), composed of listed, factory-built components, designed for open, non-enclosed use at specified minimum clearances to combustibles, and assembled in accordance with the terms of its listing to form the completed chimney. [**211**, 2010]

3.3.9.1.2 *Factory-Built, Medium-Heat Appliance–Type Chimney.* A chimney used with appliances that produce maximum flue gas temperatures of 1800°F (982°C), composed of listed, factory-built components, suitable for open, non-enclosed use at specified minimum clearances to combustibles, and assembled in accordance with the terms of the listing to form the completed chimney. [**211**, 2010]

3.3.9.1.3 *Factory Built, Residential-Type and Building Heating Appliance–Type Chimney.* A chimney suitable for continuous use at 1000°F (538°C), which complies with the 10–minute 1700°F (927°C) temperature test of ANSI/UL 103, *Standard for Factory-Built Chimneys for Residential Type and Building Heating Appliances*, and is composed of listed, factory-built components that might be fully enclosed in combustible, residential-type construction, and that is assembled in accordance with the terms of the listing to form the completed chimney. [**211**, 2010]

3.3.9.1.4 *Unlisted Metal (Smokestack) Chimney.* A manufactured or field-constructed chimney intended only for non-residential applications, having one or more metal walls or made of metal with a refractory lining, that is capable of withstanding the flue gas conditions of its use. [**211**, 2010]

3.3.9.2 *Masonry Chimney.* A field-constructed chimney of solid masonry units, bricks, stones, listed masonry chimney units, or reinforced portland cement concrete lined with suitable chimney flue liners and built in accordance with the provisions of Chapter 7 of NFPA 211, *Standard for Chimneys, Fireplaces, Vents, and Solid Fuel–Burning Appliances*. [**211**, 2010]

3.3.10 **Chimney Connector.** The pipe that connects a fuel-burning appliance to a chimney. [**211**, 2010]

3.3.11 **Chimney Flue.** The passage in a chimney for conveying the flue gases to the outside atmosphere. [**211**, 2010]

3.3.12 **Clearance.** The distance between a heat-producing appliance, chimney, chimney connector, vent, vent connector, or plenum and other surfaces.

3.3.13 **Combustible Material.** Any material that will burn, regardless of its autoignition temperature.

3.3.14 **Confined Space.** For the purposes of this standard, a space whose volume is less than 50 ft^3 per 1000 Btu/hr (4.8 m^3 per kW) of the aggregate input rating of all appliances installed in that space.

3.3.15 **Constant-Level Valve.** A device for maintaining a constant level of oil fuel within a reservoir for delivery to an oil burner.

3.3.16 Control.

3.3.16.1 *Limit Control.* An automatic safety control that responds to changes in fluid flow, fluid level, pressure, or temperature, which is normally set beyond the operating range to limit the operation of the controlled equipment by shutting off the energy supply.

3.3.16.2 *Primary Safety (Combustion Safeguard) Control.* A safety control that responds directly to flame properties, senses the presence or absence of flame, and, in the event of ignition failure or unintentional flame extinguishment, causes safety shutdown.

3.3.16.3 *Safety Control.* Automatic controls (including relays, switches, and other auxiliary equipment used in conjunction to form a safety control system) that are intended to prevent unsafe operation of the controlled equipment.

3.3.17 **Cooking Appliance, Floor-Mounted Restaurant-Type.** A range, oven, broiler, or other miscellaneous cooking appliance, designated for use in hotel and restaurant kitchens and for mounting on the floor.

3.3.18 **Damper.** A valve or plate for controlling draft or the flow of gases, including air.

3.3.19 **Dew Point.** As applied to the combustion products produced by oil-burning appliances, the temperature below which components of the combustion products will condense on exposed surfaces.

3.3.19.1 *Acid Dew Point.* The temperature below which sulfuric acid in the combustion products will condense on exposed surfaces.

3.3.19.2 *Water Dew Point.* The temperature below which water in the combustion products will condense on exposed surfaces.

3.3.20 **Direct-Fired Appliance.** A fuel-burning appliance in which the products of combustion (flue gases) are mixed with the medium (e.g., air) being heated.

3.3.21 **Direct Vent Appliance (Direct Vent System, Sealed Combustion System Appliance).** A system consisting of an appliance, combustion air and flue gas connections between the appliance and the outside atmosphere, and a vent cap supplied by the manufacturer, constructed so that all air for combustion and draft control is obtained from the outside atmosphere and all flue gases are discharged to the outside atmosphere.

3.3.22 **Direct Vent System.** See 3.3.21, Direct Vent Appliance.

3.3.23 Direct Venting System. A venting system that is constructed and installed so that air for combustion and draft control is taken from interior building spaces and all combustion products are discharged to the outside atmosphere.

3.3.24 Draft. A pressure difference that causes gases or air to flow through a chimney, vent, flue, or appliance. [**54**, 2009]

3.3.24.1* *Mechanical Draft.* Draft produced by mechanical means.

3.3.24.2 *Natural Draft.* Draft produced by the difference in the weight of a column of flue gases within a chimney or vent system and a corresponding column of air of equal dimension outside the chimney or venting system.

3.3.25 Draft Fan. A mechanical means used with a chimney venting system to augment the natural draft developed in the connected chimney.

3.3.26 Draft Regulator (Barometric). A device built into a fuel-burning appliance or made a part of a chimney connector or vent connector that functions to maintain draft through an appliance to a desired value by admitting ambient air into the appliance chimney, chimney connector, vent, or vent connector.

3.3.27 Flue Collar. That portion of an appliance designed for attachment of a chimney or vent connector or a draft hood. [**211**, 2010]

3.3.28 Furnace.

3.3.28.1 *Central Warm-Air, Forced-Air-Type Furnace.* A central furnace equipped with a blower that provides the primary means for the circulation of air. [**211**, 2010]

3.3.28.1.1 *Central Warm-Air, Forced-Air, Attic-Type Furnace.* A forced-air-type furnace designed specifically for installation in an attic or in a space with low headroom that is normally occupied. [**211**, 2010]

3.3.28.1.2 *Central Warm-Air, Forced-Air, Downflow-Type Furnace.* A forced-air-type furnace designed with airflow essentially in a vertical path, discharging air at or near the bottom of the furnace. [**211**, 2010]

3.3.28.1.3 *Central Warm-Air, Forced-Air, Horizontal-Type Furnace.* A forced-air-type furnace designed with airflow through the furnace essentially in a horizontal path. [**211**, 2010]

3.3.28.1.4 *Central Warm-Air, Forced-Air, Upflow-Type Furnace.* A forced-air-type furnace designed with airflow essentially in a vertical path, discharging air at or near the top of the furnace. [**211**, 2010]

3.3.28.2 *Central Warm-Air Furnace.* A self-contained indirect-fired or electrically heated appliance designed to supply heated air through ducts to spaces remote from or adjacent to the appliance location. [**211**, 2010]

3.3.28.3 *Central Warm-Air, Gravity-Type Furnace.* A central furnace depending primarily on circulation of air by gravity. [**211**, 2010]

3.3.28.4 *Central Warm-Air, Gravity-Type Furnace with Booster Fan.* A central furnace equipped with a booster fan that does not materially restrict free circulation of air by gravity flow when such a fan is not in operation. [**211**, 2010]

3.3.28.5 *Central Warm-Air, Gravity-Type Furnace with Integral Fan.* A central furnace equipped with a fan as an integral part of its construction and operable on gravity systems only where the fan is used only to overcome the internal resistance to airflow. [**211**, 2010]

3.3.28.6 *Duct Furnace.* A central furnace designed for installation in a duct of an air distribution system to supply warm air for heating and that depends on a blower not furnished as part of the furnace for air circulation. [**211**, 2010].

3.3.28.7* *Floor Furnace.* A self-contained indirect-fired or electrically heated furnace designed to be suspended from the floor of the space to be heated. [**211**, 2010]

3.3.28.8 *Stationary Industrial Furnace.* A low-, medium-, or high-heat appliance classified in accordance with its character and size and the temperatures developed in the portions thereof where substances or materials are heated for baking, drying, roasting, melting, vaporizing, or other purposes.

3.3.29 Heat Reclaimer, Chimney Connector–Type. A heat exchanger intended to be installed in a chimney connector between a heating appliance and the chimney to transfer heat from the flue gases through metal to air or water. [**211**, 2010]

3.3.30* Heating and Cooking Appliance. An oil-fired appliance not intended for central heating.

3.3.31 Heating Fuel. (Syn. Bioheat®, Burner Fuel, Fuel Oil, Heating Oil, Oil Burner Fuel). For the purposes of this standard, any fuel covered by one of the following specifications for petroleum distillate fuels, with or without varying amounts of biodiesel fuel meeting the specifications of ASTM D 6751, *Standard Specification for Biodiesel Fuel Blend Stock (B100) for Middle Distillate Fuels*: (1) ASTM D 396, *Standard Specification for Fuel Oils* (2) ASTM D 3699, *Standard Specification for Kerosene*.

3.3.32 Ignition Zone. The location on the burner where ignition and combustion of the main burner fuel occurs.

3.3.33 Indirect-Fired Appliance. A fuel-burning appliance in which products of combustion (flue gases) are not mixed in the appliance with the medium (e.g., air) being heated.

3.3.34 Installation. The complete setting-in-place and readying for operation of an oil-burning appliance and its accessories and equipment.

3.3.35 Kerosene-Fired Portable Heater. An unvented, self-contained, self-supporting heater, with integral reservoir, designed to be carried from one location to another.

3.3.36 Kerosene Stove. An unvented, self-contained, self-supporting kerosene-burning range or room heater equipped with an integral fuel tank not exceeding a 2 gal (7.6 L) capacity.

3.3.37* Liquid Fuel. For the purposes of this standard, any combustible liquid used as a fuel and identified under the definition of heating fuel *(see 3.3.31)* or used oil *(see 3.3.62)*.

3.3.38 Main Burner. A device or group of devices essentially forming an integral unit for the final conveyance of fuel or a mixture of fuel and air to the combustion zone and on which combustion takes place to accomplish the function for which the appliance is designed.

3.3.39 Main Burner Flame Establishing Period. The length of time fuel is permitted to be delivered to the main burner before the flame-sensing device is required to detect the main burner flame.

3.3.40 Multiple-Fueled Appliance. An appliance that is designed and intended to burn either solid, liquid, or gaseous fuels, or a combination of these.

3.3.41* Oil Burner. A device for burning oil in heating appliances such as boilers, furnaces, water heaters, and ranges.

3.3.42* Oil-Burning Appliance (Oil-Burning Unit). An appliance equipped with one or more oil burners and all the necessary safety controls, electrical equipment, and related equipment manufactured for assembly as a complete unit.

3.3.43 Oil-Burning Equipment. An oil burner of any type, together with its tank, piping, wiring, controls, and related devices, including all oil burners, oil-fired appliances, and heating and cooking appliances, but excluding those exempted by 1.1.5.

3.3.44* Oil-Burning Stove. A self-contained, freestanding, above-the-floor, indirect-fired appliance equipped with one or more oil burners.

3.3.45 Oil-Gas-Fired Appliance. An appliance that is capable of burning fuel oils and fuel gases as a main fuel source in an alternate manner.

3.3.46 Pilot. A flame that is used to light the main burner. [**86,** 2011]

3.3.47 Pilot Flame Establishing Period. For the purposes of this standard, the length of time fuel is permitted to be delivered to a proved pilot before the flame-sensing device is required to detect the pilot flame.

3.3.48 Power Venting. The application of a mechanical means of removing combustion products to the outside atmosphere. *(See 3.3.24.1, Mechanical Draft.)*

3.3.49 Pre-Purge Period. The interval of time during burner startup in which air is introduced into the combustion chamber and the associated flue passages in such volume and manner as to completely replace the air or fuel-air mixture contained therein prior to initiating ignition.

3.3.50 Qualified Person. A person who, by possession of a recognized degree, certificate, professional standing, or skill, and who, by knowledge, training, and experience, has demonstrated the ability to deal with problems relating to a particular subject matter, work, or project. [**1451,** 2007]

3.3.51 Range. An appliance intended primarily for cooking, including roasting, baking, or broiling, or any combination of these functions.

3.3.52 Readily Accessible. Capable of being reached quickly for operation, renewal, or inspections, without requiring those to whom ready access is required to climb over or remove obstacles or to resort to portable ladders and so forth. [**70,** 2011]

3.3.53 Room Heater. A heating appliance intended for installation in the space being heated and not intended for duct connection. [**211,** 2010]

3.3.53.1* *Circulating Room Heater.* A room heater with an outer jacket surrounding the heat exchanger, arranged with openings at top and bottom so that air circulates between the heat exchanger and the outer jacket. [**211,** 2010]

3.3.53.2 *Combination Room Heater/Fireplace Stove.* A chimney-connected, solid fuel–burning room heater that is designed to be operated with the fire chamber either open or closed.

3.3.53.3 *Radiant Room Heater.* A room heater designed to transfer heat primarily by direct radiation. [**211,** 2010]

3.3.53.4 *Solid Fuel Room Heater.* A chimney-connected, solid fuel–burning room heater that is designed to be operated with the fire chamber closed. [**211,** 2010]

3.3.54 Safety Shutdown. The action of shutting off all fuel and ignition energy to an appliance by means of a safety control or controls, such that restart of the appliance cannot be accomplished without some form of manual reset that requires local, manual intervention.

3.3.55 Sealed Combustion Venting System. See 3.3.21, Direct Vent Appliance.

3.3.56 Sidewall or Through-Wall Venting. A mechanical means applied to a nearly horizontal venting system to remove combustion products without benefit of a chimney or significant natural draft.

3.3.57 Tank.

3.3.57.1* *Oil Burner Auxiliary Tank.* A tank having a capacity of not more than 60 gal (227 L) that is listed for installation in the supply piping between a burner and its main fuel supply tank. *(See 3.3.57.3, Oil Burner Integral Tank.)*

3.3.57.2 *Oil Burner Gravity Tank.* A supply tank from which the oil is delivered directly to the burner by gravity.

3.3.57.3 *Oil Burner Integral Tank.* A tank that is furnished by the manufacturer as an integral part of an oil-burning appliance. *(See 3.3.57.1, Oil Burner Auxiliary Tank.)*

3.3.57.4 *Oil Burner Storage Tank.* A separate tank that is not connected directly to the oil-burning appliance.

3.3.57.5 *Oil Burner Supply Tank.* A separate tank connected either directly or by means of a pump to the oil-burning appliance.

3.3.58 Total Input Rating. The sum of the maximum Btu rating, as marked on the appliance by the manufacturer, of all appliances, not the nozzle sizes or actual firing rates.

3.3.59 Trial for Ignition Period. The interval of time during which main burner fuel is permitted to be delivered into the ignition zone before the flame-sensing device is required to detect flame. *(See 3.3.39, Main Burner Flame Establishing Period, and 3.3.47, Pilot Flame Establishing Period.)*

3.3.60* Unconfined Space. Any space whose volume is equal to or greater than 50 ft^3 per 1000 Btu/hr (4.8 m^3 per kW) of the aggregate input rating of all fuel-burning appliances installed therein.

3.3.61* Unit Heater. A self-contained heating appliance that might or might not include an integral fan for circulating air, that can be of the floor-mounted or suspended type and that is intended for the heating of the space in which it is installed.

3.3.62 Used Oil. Oil that consists of primarily used automotive crankcase oil from internal combustion engines, including, but not limited to, used engine oils, used automotive transmission fluids, used gear lubricants, machining oils, used hydraulic fluids, or any mixture thereof and that can vary considerably in its chemical and physical properties.

3.3.63 Valve.

3.3.63.1 *Manual Oil Shutoff Valve.* A manually operated valve in an oil line for the purpose of turning on or completely shutting off the oil supply to the burner.

3.3.63.2 *Metering (Regulating) Valve.* An oil control valve for regulating burner input.

3.3.63.3 *Oil Control Valve.* An automatically or manually operated device consisting essentially of an oil valve for controlling the fuel supply to a burner.

3.3.63.4 *Safety Valve.* An automatic oil control valve of the "on" and "off" type (without any bypass to the burner) that is actuated by a safety control or by an emergency device.

3.3.64 Vent, Type L. A vertical or nearly vertical passageway composed of listed factory-built components assembled in accordance with the terms of listing for conveying flue gases from oil and gas appliances or their vent connectors to the outside atmosphere.

3.3.65* Venting System (Flue Gases). A continuous, open passageway from the flue collar or draft hood of a fuel-burning appliance to the outside atmosphere for the purpose of removing flue gases. [**211,** 2010]

3.3.66* Wall Furnace. A self-contained vented appliance, complete with grilles or equivalent, designed for incorporation in or permanent attachment to the structure of a building, manufactured home, or recreational vehicle and furnishing heated air directly into the space to be heated through openings in the casing.

3.3.66.1 *Fan-Type Wall Furnace.* A wall furnace equipped with a fan for the circulation of air.

3.3.66.2 *Gravity-Type Wall Furnace.* A wall furnace dependent on the circulation of air by gravity.

3.3.67 Water Heater. A fuel-burning appliance for heating water to a temperature not more than 200°F (93°C). [**211,** 2010]

Chapter 4 Basic Installation and Operation Requirements

4.1 Scope. This chapter shall apply to the basic installation and operation requirements for oil-burning appliances and equipment.

4.2 Use of Approved Equipment.

4.2.1 Oil-burning appliances and equipment shall be approved.

4.2.2 Appliances and equipment listed for a specific purpose shall be considered as meeting the requirements of this standard.

4.3 Installation of Oil-Burning Appliances and Equipment.

4.3.1 Before installing or remodeling any oil-burning appliance or equipment for commercial or industrial application, plans or sketches that show the relative location of burners, tanks, pumps, piping, and elevations of buildings and their lowest floors or pits relating to the proposed installation or alteration shall be submitted to the authority having jurisdiction.

4.3.2 The installation shall be made in accordance with manufacturers' instructions, as well as in accordance with all federal, state, and local rules and regulations.

4.3.2.1 Such instructions shall include directions and information for attaining proper and safe installation, maintenance, and use of the appliance or equipment.

4.3.2.2 The instructions shall be left with the owner.

4.3.2.3 If for any reason it becomes necessary to change, modify, or alter a manufacturer's instructions in any way, written approval shall be obtained from the manufacturer before doing so.

4.3.3 The installation shall be made by qualified, competent technicians experienced in making such installations.

4.3.4 The installation shall be accessible for cleaning heating surfaces; for removing burners; for replacing motors, controls, air filters, chimney connectors, draft regulators, and other working parts; and for adjusting, cleaning, and lubricating parts requiring such attention.

4.3.5 Oil-burning appliances shall not be installed or located in areas where combustible dusts or flammable liquids, gases, or vapors are normally present.

4.3.5.1 Return air for warm air units shall not be taken from such areas.

4.3.6 Oil-burning appliances and equipment shall be installed so that a minimum 3 ft (0.9 m) separation is maintained from any electrical panelboard and a minimum 5 ft (1.5 m) separation is maintained from any unenclosed fuel oil tank.

4.3.7 After installation, the appliance or equipment shall be tested for proper operation and combustion performance to make certain that the burner is operating in a safe and acceptable manner and that all accessory equipment, controls, and safety devices function as intended.

4.3.8 Contractors installing industrial oil-burning systems shall furnish diagrams showing the main oil lines and control valves, one of which shall be posted at the equipment and another at some point that will be readily accessible in case of emergency.

4.3.9 After completing the installation, the installer shall instruct the owner or operator on the proper operation of the equipment.

4.3.9.1 The installer also shall furnish the owner or operator with name(s) and telephone numbers of person(s) to contact for technical information or assistance and for routine or emergency services.

4.4 Electrical Services.

4.4.1 Electrical wiring and utilization equipment used in connection with oil-burning appliances or equipment shall be installed in accordance with *NFPA 70, National Electrical Code.*

4.4.2 Safety control circuits shall be 2-wire, one side grounded, with a nominal voltage not exceeding 150 volts.

4.4.3 Safety controls or protective devices shall be connected so that they interrupt the ungrounded conductor and shut all fuel flow to the appliance, including fuel flow to any pilot flame or burner.

4.4.4 The control circuit shall be connected to a power supply branch circuit fused at not more than the value appropriate for the rating of any control or device included in the circuit.

4.5 Acceptable Liquid Fuels.

4.5.1* The type and grade of liquid fuel used in a liquid fuel–burning appliance shall be that liquid fuel for which the appliance is listed and approved or is stipulated by the manufacturer. Liquid fuels shall meet one of the following specifications and shall not contain gasoline or any other flammable liquid:

(1) ASTM D 396, *Standard Specification for Fuel Oils*
(2) ASTM D 3699, *Standard Specification for Kerosene*
(3) ASTM D 6448, *Industrial Burner Fuels from Used Lube Oils*
(4) ASTM D 6751, *Standard Specification for Biodiesel Fuel Blend Stock (B100) for Middle Distillate Fuel*
(5) ASTM D 6823, *Commercial Burner Fuels from Used Lube Oils*

4.5.2 Crankcase oil or used oil shall not be used as fuel unless all of the following conditions are met:

(1) The installation is in a commercial or industrial occupancy.
(2) The oil-burning appliance is designed to burn crankcase oil or used oil and is listed for such use.

(3) The appliance is installed in accordance with the manufacturer's instructions and with the terms of its listing.

(4) The installation meets the applicable requirements of Section 4.6 and Chapter 12.

4.5.3* Where heavy oils are used, the following shall be required:

(1) The oil-burning appliance shall be designed to burn such fuels.

(2) Means shall be provided to maintain the oil at its proper atomizing temperature.

(3) Automatically operated burners that require preheating of oil shall be arranged so that no oil can be delivered for combustion until the oil is at the proper atomizing temperature.

(4)*Use of an oil-fired appliance that is listed in accordance with ANSI/UL 296A, *Standard for Waste Oil-Burning Air-Heating Appliances,* shall be deemed as meeting the intent of 4.5.3(1) through 4.5.3(3).

4.5.4 A properly sized and rated oil filter or strainer shall be installed in the oil supply line to an oil burner.

4.6 Use of Crankcase Oil and Used Oil.

4.6.1* During any storing, handling, or burning of crankcase oil and used oils, care shall be taken to not mix gasoline with the crankcase oil or used oil.

4.6.2 When a mixture could have a flash point below 100°F (38°C) or when a mixture could be heated above its flash point, attention shall be given to electrical installations in areas where flammable vapors or gases can be present in the atmosphere.

4.6.3 Where a supply tank is used, provisions shall be made to prevent stratification of fuel in the tank.

4.6.4* Areas where oil leakage can occur, such as at pumps, heaters, strainers, and burners, or where maintenance is performed shall be provided with adequate ventilation. Confined fuel-handling areas and burner sites shall also be provided with adequate ventilation. Mechanical ventilation shall be provided where necessary.

4.6.5 Means shall be provided to safely dispose of spills.

4.7 Temporary Heating. Where salamanders, space heaters, or other heating appliances are used for temporary heating, all requirements of this standard, including those for maximum operating temperatures, clearances to combustible materials, venting of combustion gases, fuel storage, safety, shut-offs, combustion and ventilation air, and electrical wiring, where applicable, shall be met and all such equipment shall be used in accordance with its listing.

Chapter 5   Air for Combustion and Ventilation

5.1 Scope. This chapter shall apply to those requirements necessary to ensure that adequate air for safe combustion is provided for oil-burning appliances and equipment.

5.2 Basic Requirements.

5.2.1 Oil-burning appliances and equipment shall be installed in locations where available ventilation permits satisfactory combustion of oil, proper venting of combustion gases, and maintenance of safe ambient temperatures under normal conditions of use.

5.2.2 Appliances shall be located so that they do not interfere with the supply of air within the space.

5.2.3 Where buildings are so tight that normal infiltration does not provide sufficient air for combustion, outside air shall be introduced.

5.2.3.1 Ducts used to convey air from outdoors shall have the same cross-sectional area as the free area of the openings to which they connect.

5.2.3.2 The smaller dimension of rectangular air ducts shall not be less than 3 in. (75 mm).

5.2.4 For residential and similar installations, the requirements of 5.2.1 shall be permitted to be met by application of either one of the methods covered in Section 5.3 or Section 5.4. For commercial and industrial installations, the requirements of Section 5.5 shall apply.

5.3 Appliances Located in Unconfined Spaces.

5.3.1* In unconfined spaces in buildings of conventional frame, brick, or stone construction, air for combustion and ventilation shall be permitted to be supplied by normal infiltration.

5.3.2 If normal infiltration is not sufficient because of tight construction, air for combustion and ventilation shall be obtained directly from outdoors or from spaces that freely communicate with outdoors by means of a permanent opening or openings having a total free area of not less than 1 in.^{2} per 5000 Btu/hr (28 in.^{2} per gal/hr) (4.4 cm^2/kW), based on the total input rating of all appliances in the space.

5.4 Appliances Located in Confined Spaces. For appliances installed in confined spaces, air for combustion and ventilation shall be provided using one of the methods set forth in this section.

5.4.1 All Air Taken from Inside the Building.

5.4.1.1 The confined space shall be provided with two permanent openings as shown in Figure 5.4.1.1, one near the top of the space and one near the bottom.

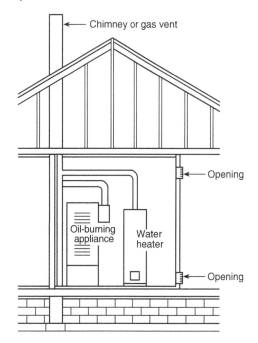

FIGURE 5.4.1.1 Appliances Located in Confined Spaces — All Air Taken from Inside the Building.

5.4.1.2 Each opening shall have a free area of not less than 1 in.^{2} per 1000 Btu/hr (140 in.^{2} per gal/hr) (22 cm^2/kW), based on the total input rating of all appliances in the space.

5.4.1.3 Each opening shall freely communicate with interior areas of the building that, in turn, have adequate infiltration from the outside.

5.4.2 All Air Taken from Outdoors.

5.4.2.1 The confined space shall be provided with two permanent openings, one in or near the top of the space and one in or near the bottom.

5.4.2.2 The openings shall communicate directly or by means of ducts with the outdoors or to spaces, such as an attic or crawl space, that themselves freely communicate with the outdoors, as shown in Figure 5.4.2.2(a), Figure 5.4.2.2(b), and Figure 5.4.2.2(c).

5.4.2.3 Where communicating with the outdoors directly or by means of vertical ducts, each opening shall have a free area of not less than 1 in.^{2} per 4000 Btu/hr (35 in.^{2} per gal/hr) (5.5 cm^2/kW), based on the total input rating of all appliances in the space.

5.4.2.4 Where communicating with the outdoors by means of horizontal ducts, each opening shall have a free area of not less than 1 in.^{2} per 2000 Btu/hr (70 in.^{2} per gal/hr) (11 cm^2/kW), based on the total input rating of all appliances in the space.

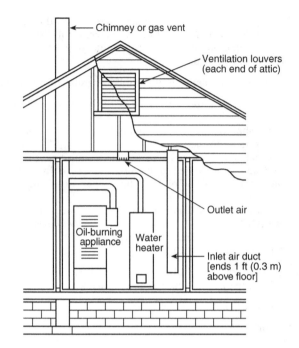

FIGURE 5.4.2.2(b) Appliances Located in Confined Spaces — All Air from Outdoors Through Ventilated Attic.

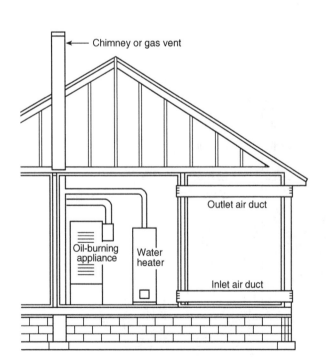

FIGURE 5.4.2.2(a) Appliances Located in Confined Spaces — All Air from Outdoors.

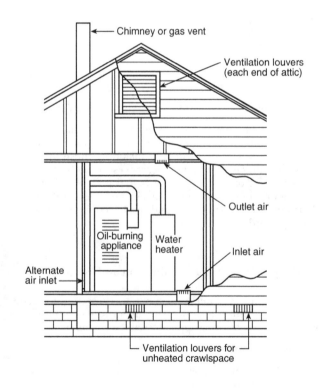

FIGURE 5.4.2.2(c) Appliances Located in Confined Spaces — All Air from Outdoors, with Inlet Air from Ventilated Crawl Space and Outlet Air to Ventilated Attic.

5.4.3 Ventilation Air Taken from Inside the Building — Combustion Air Taken from Outdoors.

5.4.3.1 The confined space shall be provided with two openings for ventilation, located and sized as specified in 5.4.1 and as shown in Figure 5.4.3.1.

5.4.3.2 In addition, there shall be one opening communicating directly with the outdoors or to spaces, such as an attic or crawl space, that freely communicates with the outdoors and has a free area of not less than 1 in.^{2} per 5000 Btu/hr (28 in.^{2} per gal/hr) (4.4 cm^2/kW), based on the total input of all appliances in the space.

5.5 Combustion Air for Commercial and Industrial Installations. For commercial and industrial oil-burning equipment, permanent means for supplying an ample amount of outside air shall be provided in accordance with this section.

5.5.1 For furnace or boiler rooms adjacent to outside walls and where combustion air is provided by natural ventilation from the outside, there shall be a permanent air supply inlet having a total free area of not less than 1 in.^{2} per 4000 Btu/hr (35 in.^{2} per gal/hr) (5.5 cm^2/kW), based on the total input rating of the burner or burners, but in no case less than 35 in.^{2} (0.425 m^2).

5.5.2 For furnace or boiler rooms that are not adjacent to outside walls, the combustion air shall be supplied in a manner acceptable to the authority having jurisdiction.

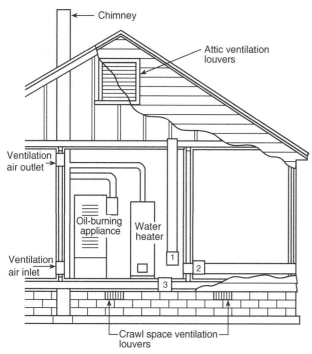

Note: Ducts used for make-up air can be connected to the cold air return of the heating system only if they connect directly to outdoor air.

Nos. 1, 2, and 3 mark alternate locations for air from outdoors.

Provide attic ventilation louvers at each end of attic with alternate air inlet No. 1.

Provide crawl space ventilation louvers for unheated crawl space with alternate air inlet No. 3.

FIGURE 5.4.3.1 Appliances Located in Confined Spaces, with Ventilation Air from Inside Building and Combustion Air from Outside, Ventilated Attic, or Ventilated Crawl Space.

5.6 Louvers and Grilles.

5.6.1 In calculating the free area required by Sections 5.2, 5.3, 5.4, and 5.5, the blocking effect of louvers, grilles, or screens protecting openings shall be taken into consideration.

5.6.2 Screens used in louvers or grilles shall not be smaller than ¼ in. (6.3 mm) mesh and shall be accessible for cleaning.

5.6.3 If the free area through a particular design of louver or grille is known, it shall be used in calculating the size of the opening needed to provide the free area required. If the free area of the design is not known, it shall be assumed that wood louvers will have 20 percent to 25 percent free area and metal louvers and grilles will have 60 percent to 75 percent free area.

5.7 Special Conditions. Where an appliance is installed in a location where the operation of exhaust fans, kitchen ventilation systems, clothes dryers, or fireplaces can create conditions of unsatisfactory combustion or venting, special provisions shall be made subject to the approval of the authority having jurisdiction.

5.8* Specially Engineered Installations. The size of combustion air openings required by Sections 5.3, 5.4, and 5.5 shall not govern when special engineering methods approved by the authority having jurisdiction ensure an adequate supply of air for combustion and ventilation.

Chapter 6   Venting of Combustion (Flue) Gases

6.1 Scope. This chapter shall apply to those requirements necessary to ensure the safe venting of combustion and flue gases from oil-burning appliances and equipment.

6.2 Basic Requirements.

6.2.1 Oil-burning appliances and equipment other than direct-fired heaters, listed kerosene stoves, and listed portable kerosene heaters shall be connected to venting systems and chimneys to remove combustion (flue) gases from the combustion chamber of the appliance or equipment and to direct them to a point outside the building, as required by this chapter.

Exception: As provided for in Section 6.7.

6.2.2 The installation of oil-burning appliances and equipment shall require careful consideration of positive and negative pressures in the venting system and chimney and the formation of corrosive condensate throughout the system.

6.2.3 The venting system and chimney shall be designed, constructed, and maintained to ensure that a positive flow is developed and that this flow is sufficient to remove products of combustion to the outside atmosphere.

6.3 Draft.

6.3.1* A chimney shall be capable of producing the minimum draft recommended by the manufacturer of the appliance.

6.3.2 A draft fan, installed so that the fuel supply to the main burner is immediately shut off if the draft fan fails, shall be permitted to be used to increase low draft.

6.3.3 Two or more oil-burning appliances shall be permitted to be connected to a single chimney, provided that sufficient draft is available for safe combustion in each appliance and that all products of combustion are safely removed to the outdoors.

6.3.4* Where chimney downdraft conditions cause faulty operation that creates a hazard, corrective steps shall be taken.

6.4 Draft Regulators.

6.4.1 A draft regulator shall be provided for each oil-burning appliance that is connected to a chimney or power venting system unless the appliance design, conditions of installation, or combinations thereof preclude excessive chimney draft, or the appliance is listed for use without one.

6.4.2 A manually operated damper shall not be placed in the chimney connector from an oil-burning appliance.

Exception: Where two or more oil-burning appliances are connected to a common chimney, manual isolating dampers shall be permitted and shall be interlocked to prevent burner operation unless the damper is in the full-open position.

6.4.3 Automatically operated dampers shall be of an approved type, shall be designed to maintain a safe damper opening at all times, and shall be arranged to prevent starting of the burner unless the damper is fully opened.

6.4.4 Fixed baffles shall be permitted to be installed in the appliance flue collar where they are specified by the appliance manufacturer.

6.4.4.1 Baffles shall be securely fastened into position. When in a closed position, baffles shall not block off more than 80 percent of the chimney connector area.

6.5 Chimney Connectors.

6.5.1 An oil-burning appliance shall be placed so that the chimney connector is as short as practicable.

6.5.1.1 For natural-draft appliances, the horizontal length of a chimney connector shall not exceed 10 ft (3 m) unless a draft fan is used.

6.5.1.2 For appliances requiring a negative chimney draft, the chimney connector shall be not longer than 75 percent of the portion of the chimney above the chimney connector inlet.

6.5.2 A chimney connector shall not pass through a floor or ceiling.

6.5.3 A chimney connector of a low-, medium-, or high-heat industrial appliance shall not pass through a combustible wall or partition.

6.5.4 Chimney connectors of appliances other than industrial appliances shall not pass through combustible walls or partitions unless the installation complies with 6.5.4.1, 6.5.4.2, or 6.5.4.3.

6.5.4.1 Chimney connectors shall be permitted to pass through a combustible wall or partition if guarded at the point of passage by one of the following:

(1) Metal ventilated thimbles not less than 12 in. (300 mm) larger in diameter than the diameter of the connector
(2) Metal or burned fire-clay thimbles built in brickwork or other approved fireproofing materials and extending not less than 8 in. (200 mm) beyond all sides of the thimble

6.5.4.2 Chimney connectors shall be permitted to pass through a combustible wall or partition if all combustible material in the wall or partition is cut away from the chimney connector a sufficient distance to provide the clearance required from the connector and noncombustible insulating material is used to close up the opening.

6.5.4.3 Chimney connectors shall be permitted to pass through a combustible wall or partition if a listed, commercially available or factory-built vent assembly, such as a Type L vent, that is approved for use with oil-fired appliances is used.

6.5.5 In masonry chimneys, the chimney connector shall extend through the chimney wall to the inner face or liner, but not beyond, and shall be firmly cemented in place.

6.5.5.1 A thimble shall be permitted to be used to facilitate removal of the chimney connector for cleaning, in which case the thimble shall be permanently cemented in place with high-temperature cement.

6.5.6 The chimney connector shall be sized in accordance with one of the following methods:

(1) The connector shall be sized using approved engineering methods, and the connected appliance shall be marked to indicate the maximum firing rate that can be used with the venting system.
(2) The connector shall be sized in accordance with the manufacturer's instructions.

6.5.7 The connector, for its entire length, shall not be smaller in effective cross-sectional area than the flue collar of the appliance, as delivered or as modified in accordance with the manufacturer's instructions. Any change in size made to accommodate a chimney lining system shall be done at the connection to that system.

6.5.8 The chimney connector shall be of steel, refractory masonry, or corrosion-resistant material and shall be maintained in good condition.

6.5.9 Where insulation of the chimney connector is required to maintain the temperature of the combustion products, an insulated Type L chimney connector or a factory-built chimney connector listed for that purpose shall be used.

6.5.10 The chimney connector shall maintain a pitch or rise of at least ¼ in./ft (20 mm/m) of horizontal length of pipe from the appliance to the chimney.

6.5.11 The chimney connector shall be installed to minimize the number of elbows and to avoid sharp turns or other construction features that might create excessive resistance to the flow of flue gases.

6.5.12 Any device that will obstruct the free flow of gases shall not be installed in a chimney connector or chimney.

Exception: This requirement shall not be construed as prohibiting the use of devices specifically listed for installation in a chimney connector, such as heat reclaimers, automatic dampers, or safety controls.

6.5.13 The chimney connector shall be securely supported.

6.5.14 Each joint of the chimney connector shall be fastened together with at least three screws.

6.5.15 Clearance from combustible construction or materials shall be as specified in Table 10.6.1, except as permitted by 6.5.4 and Table 10.6.2.

6.5.16 The entire length of the chimney connector shall be accessible for inspection, cleaning, and replacement.

6.5.17 Placement of the chimney connector shall maintain minimum fire protection clearances.

6.5.18 A connector shall not be connected to a chimney flue serving a fireplace unless the fireplace opening is sealed or the chimney flue that vents the fireplace is permanently sealed below the connection.

6.5.19 Connectors serving appliances operating under natural draft shall not be connected into any portion of a mechanical draft system operating under a positive pressure.

6.5.20 Connectors for appliances installed in attics or crawl spaces shall be either a Type L chimney connector or a factory-built chimney connector listed for the purpose, or the appliance shall be attached directly to the chimney.

6.5.21 If two or more openings are provided into a chimney flue, they shall be at different levels and the smaller connector shall enter at the higher level consistent with available head room or clearance to combustible material. [**211**:9.8.4]

6.5.22 Regardless of the fuel(s) used, two or more connectors shall not be joined unless the common connector, the manifold, and the chimney are sized to serve the appliances connected thereto.

6.5.22.1 Adequate draft shall be available to remove all products of combustion to the outdoors without leakage, spillage, or backflow from the connectors, manifold, chimney, or appliances.

6.5.23 Two or more oil-burning appliances shall be permitted to be connected to a common venting system, provided the following conditions are met:

(1) Each appliance is equipped with a primary safety control.
(2) The venting system is designed to meet the requirements of the applicable code.

6.5.24 Oil-burning appliances that are connected to a common venting system shall be located within the same story of the building unless the vent system is specifically designed for the purpose and has been approved by the authority having jurisdiction.

6.5.25 Solid fuel–burning appliances shall not be connected to a chimney flue serving another appliance burning other fuels, unless specifically listed for such connection.

6.5.26 Gas utilization appliances and appliances burning liquid fuel shall be permitted to be connected to the same chimney flue through separate openings.

6.5.27 Gas utilization appliances and appliances burning liquid fuel shall be permitted to be connected to the same chimney flue through a single opening, provided the appliances are joined by a suitable fitting located as close as practicable to the chimney and provided the following conditions are met:

(1) Sufficient draft is available for the safe combustion of each appliance and for the removal of all products of combustion. [**211**:9.8.3(1)]
(2) The appliances so connected are equipped with primary safety controls. [**211**:9.8.3(2)]

6.5.28 Single-wall connector pipe shall be installed by one of the following methods:

(1) In accordance with the appliance manufacturer's instructions
(2) With the crimped end toward the chimney

6.5.29 The minimum thickness for steel pipe connectors shall meet the requirements of Table 6.5.29.

Table 6.5.29 Minimum Thickness for Steel Pipe Connectors

Pipe Diameter (in.)	Sheet Metal Gauge
Up to 9	26
>9 up to 10	24
>10 up to 16	22
>16	16

For SI units, 1 in. = 25 mm.

6.6 Chimneys.

6.6.1 Masonry and metal chimneys shall be erected in accordance with applicable building code requirements.

6.6.2 Masonry chimneys shall meet the requirements of Chapter 7 of NFPA 211, *Standard for Chimneys, Fireplaces, Vents, and Solid Fuel–Burning Appliances.*

6.6.3 Metal chimneys shall meet the requirements of Chapter 8 of NFPA 211, *Standard for Chimneys, Fireplaces, Vents, and Solid Fuel–Burning Appliances.*

6.6.4 Factory-built chimneys shall be listed, installed, and used in accordance with their listings and with manufacturers' instructions.

6.6.5 Factory-built chimneys shall meet the requirements of Chapter 6 of NFPA 211, *Standard for Chimneys, Fireplaces, Vents, and Solid Fuel–Burning Appliances.*

6.6.6* The flue gas exit of a chimney shall be at least 3 ft (0.9 m) above the highest point where it passes through the roof of a building and shall be at least 2 ft (0.6 m) higher than any portion of a building within 10 ft (3 m) of the chimney.

6.6.7* Prior to the installation of a new or replacement oil burner or oil-burning appliance, the installer shall perform a visual inspection of the chimney or flue gas venting system and shall verify the proper size of the chimney or flue gas venting system. *(See Annex E for additional information.)*

6.6.7.1 The inspection shall be limited to the cleanout and to the area where the flue gas connector enters the chimney or flue gas venting system and to the extent possible with artificial lighting and conventional tools such as a mirror.

6.6.7.2 If deterioration exists or if the chimney or flue gas venting system is found to inhibit the performance of the oil burner or oil-burning appliance, as specified by the manufacturer, the owner shall be notified in writing, stating that the chimney or flue gas venting system to which the appliance is connected shall be examined by a qualified person in accordance with the requirements of Chapter 14 of NFPA 211, *Standard for Chimneys, Fireplaces, Vents, and Solid Fuel–Burning Appliances.*

6.6.8* Masonry chimneys shall be lined with an approved clay tile liner or a listed chimney lining system installed in accordance with manufacturers' instructions.

6.6.9* When chimneys are relined, the liner shall be listed or shall be of an approved material that will resist corrosion, softening, or cracking from the flue gases, at a temperature appropriate to the class of service.

6.6.10 All portions of a mechanical draft system under positive pressure during operation shall be designed and installed so as to prevent leakage of flue gas into the building.

6.7 Special Venting Systems.

6.7.1 Type L Venting Systems.

6.7.1.1 Listed Type L venting systems shall be permitted to be used with appliances that are listed as suitable for installation with Type L venting systems.

6.7.1.2 Type L venting systems shall be installed and used in accordance with their listings and the manufacturers' instructions.

6.7.1.3 A Type L venting system shall be capable of producing the minimum draft recommended by the manufacturer of the appliance.

6.7.1.4 The flue gas exit of a Type L venting system shall be at least 2 ft (0.6 m) above the highest point where it passes through the roof of a building and at least 2 ft (0.6 m) higher than any portion of a building within 10 ft (3 m) of such Type L venting system.

6.7.2 Direct Vent Appliances.

6.7.2.1 Direct vent appliances (sealed combustion system appliances) shall be listed. They shall be installed in accordance with their listing and with manufacturers' instructions.

6.7.2.2 The combustion air inlet and flue gas outlet of a direct vent appliance shall terminate in the same plane and in the same ambient pressure zone when they terminate in the outside wall of the structure.

6.7.3* Termination of Special Venting Systems.

6.7.3.1 A venting system that terminates in the sidewall of a structure shall terminate at least 3 ft (0.9 m) above any air inlet to the structure that is within 10 ft (3 m) of the termination point.

Exception No. 1: This requirement shall not apply to the combustion air intake of a direct vent appliance.

Exception No. 2: This requirement shall not apply to the separation distance between the circulating air inlet and the vent discharge of a listed outdoor appliance.

6.7.3.2 The flue gas outlet of an appliance other than a direct vent appliance shall terminate at least 4 ft (1.2 m) below, 4 ft (1.2 m) horizontally from, or 1 ft (0.3 m) above any door, window, or gravity air inlet of the structure and also shall terminate at least 1 ft (0.3 m) above grade.

6.7.3.3 The combustion air inlet and flue gas outlet of a direct vent appliance or the flue gas outlet of an appliance other than a direct vent appliance shall terminate at least 1 ft (0.3 m) from the soffit of the roof of the structure and at least 3 ft (0.9 m) from an inside corner of an L-shaped structure.

6.7.3.4 The exit terminal of a mechanical draft system shall not be less than 7 ft (2.1 m) above grade when located adjacent to public walkways.

6.7.3.5 Any air inlet and any flue gas outlet of any appliance shall terminate at least 5 ft (1.5 m) from the vent outlet of a liquid fuel supply tank.

6.8 Replacement and Upgrading of Chimneys. (Reserved)

Chapter 7   Tanks for Liquid Fuels

7.1 Scope. This chapter shall apply to tanks used to store or to supply liquid fuel for use in liquid fuel–burning appliances.

7.2 Basic Design and Construction of Tanks.

7.2.1 Tanks shall be designed and constructed to any shape or type consistent with sound engineering practice for the materials of construction used and shall be listed in accordance with one of the design standards specified in 7.2.7 or their approved equivalents.

7.2.2 Tanks shall be installed and used in accordance with this standard and shall be approved for the specific liquid fuel–burning application.

7.2.3 Tanks meeting the requirements of Chapters 21, 22, and 23 of NFPA 30, *Flammable and Combustible Liquids Code*, shall be deemed as meeting the requirements of this section.

7.2.4 Tanks shall be permitted to have combustible or noncombustible internal linings that are compatible with the intended liquid fuel(s).

7.2.5 Tank Openings for Fill and Venting.

7.2.5.1 All tanks shall be provided with top openings large enough to prevent abnormal pressures in the tank during normal operations (fill and withdrawal) and emergency venting (fire exposure for aboveground tanks), but not smaller than the nominal pipe sizes specified in Table 7.2.5.1.

Table 7.2.5.1 Minimum Diameter of Tank Vent Opening

Capacity of Tank (U.S. gal)	Diameter of Vent, Nominal Opening Size (in.)
660 or less	1¼
661 to 3,000	1½
3,001 to 10,000	2
10,001 to 20,000	2½
20,001 to 35,000	3

For SI units, 1 gal = 3.785 L, 1 in. = 25 mm.

7.2.5.2 Normal and emergency vent opening(s) shall be permitted to be either separate or combined, provided openings are sized in accordance with Table 7.2.5.1.

7.2.5.3 Interstitial spaces of secondary containment tanks shall be provided with venting sized in accordance with Table 7.2.5.1.

7.2.5.4 Each compartment of a compartmented tank shall be provided with venting sized in accordance with Table 7.2.5.1.

7.2.6 Operating Pressures.

7.2.6.1 Tanks shall be permitted to be operated under normal operating conditions at pressures that do not exceed a gauge pressure of 1 psi (gauge pressure of 7 kPa), measured at the top of the tank, but shall be limited to a gauge pressure of 2.5 psi (gauge pressure of 17 kPa) under emergency venting conditions, also measured at the top of the tank.

7.2.6.2 Where the vertical length of the fill and vent pipes is such that the static head imposed on the bottom of the tank exceeds a gauge pressure of 10 psi (70 kPa) if the pipes are filled with liquid, the tank and its related piping shall be tested hydrostatically to a pressure equal to the static head thus imposed.

7.2.7 Design Standards.

7.2.7.1 Atmospheric tanks shall be constructed in accordance with one of the following or its approved equivalent:

(1) API Standard 650, *Specifications for Welded Steel Tanks for Oil Storage*
(2) UL 58, *Standard for Steel Underground Tanks for Flammable and Combustible Liquids*
(3) ANSI/UL 80, *Standard for Steel Tanks for Oil-Burner Fuels and Other Combustible Liquids*
(4) ANSI/UL 142, *Standard for Steel Aboveground Tanks for Flammable and Combustible Liquids*
(5) ANSI/UL 443, *Standard for Steel Auxiliary Tanks for Oil Burner Fuel*
(6) UL 1316, *Standard for Glass-Fiber-Reinforced Plastic Underground Storage Tanks for Petroleum Products, Alcohols, and Alcohol–Gasoline Mixtures*
(7) ANSI/UL 1746, *Standard for External Corrosion Protection Systems for Steel Underground Storage Tanks*
(8) UL 2080, *Standard for Fire Resistant Tanks for Flammable and Combustible Liquids*
(9) ANSI/UL 2085, *Standard for Protected Aboveground Tanks for Flammable and Combustible Liquids*
(10) UL 2245, *Standard for Below-Grade Vaults for Flammable Liquid Storage Tanks*
(11) SU 2258, *Outline of Investigation for Nonmetallic Tanks for Oil Burner Fuels and Other Combustible Liquids*

7.2.7.2 Tanks intended for use inside buildings and with a capacity between 10 gal (38 L) and 1320 gal (5000 L) shall be constructed in accordance with 7.2.7.1(3), 7.2.7.1(4), 7.2.7.1(5), 7.2.7.1(8), 7.2.7.1(9), or 7.2.7.1(11).

7.2.7.3 Tanks intended for use inside buildings and with a capacity greater than 1320 gal (5000 L) shall be constructed in accordance with 7.2.7.1(4), 7.2.7.1(8), or 7.2.7.1(9).

7.2.7.4 Tanks intended for use outside aboveground with a capacity no greater than 1320 gal (5000 L) shall be constructed in accordance with 7.2.7.1(3), 7.2.7.1(4), 7.2.7.1(8), 7.2.7.1(9), or 7.2.7.1(11).

7.2.7.5 Tanks intended for use outside aboveground with a capacity greater than 1320 gal (5000 L) shall be constructed in accordance with 7.2.7.1(1), 7.2.7.1(4), 7.2.7.1(8), or 7.2.7.1(9).

7.2.7.6* Tanks intended for use underground shall be constructed in accordance with 7.2.7.1(2), 7.2.7.1(6), or 7.2.7.1(7). Tanks constructed in accordance with 7.2.7.1(2) shall be protected in accordance with either of the following:

(1) An approved cathodic protection system that is engineered, installed, and maintained in accordance with recognized standards
(2) Approved or listed external corrosion-resistant systems or materials integral with the tank

7.2.7.7* If a tank is installed in a vault outside the building, either above or below grade, the vault shall be constructed in accordance with 7.2.7.1(10).

7.2.8 Areas Subject to Flood or Earthquake. Where a tank is located in an area that is designated as subject to flood or earthquake, the following additional requirements shall apply

to the tank, its connections, and its foundation and supports, as appropriate.

7.2.8.1 When in a designated flood zone, the requirements of NFPA 30, *Flammable and Combustible Liquids Code*, or local requirements shall be met.

7.2.8.2 When in a designated seismic zone, the local requirements for earthquake resistance shall be met.

7.3 Supports and Foundations.

7.3.1* Tanks and their supports shall rest on foundations made of solid concrete.

7.3.2 The tank foundation shall be designed to minimize uneven settling and to minimize corrosion in any part of the tank resting on the foundation.

7.3.3 The tank supports shall be integral to the tank or shall be of concrete, solid masonry, or steel. For outside aboveground tanks, the supports shall be firmly anchored to the foundation.

7.3.4 Steel supports for any outside aboveground tank whose capacity exceeds 660 gal (2500 L) shall be considered protected if they meet one of the following methods and are approved by the authority having jurisdiction:

(1) They are protected by materials having a fire resistance rating of not less than 2 hours.
(2) They are not otherwise protected, but are less than 12 in. (0.3 m) high at their lowest point.
(3) They are protected by a water spray system that meets the requirements of NFPA 15, *Standard for Water Spray Fixed Systems for Fire Protection*, or NFPA 13, *Standard for the Installation of Sprinkler Systems*.

7.3.5 Every tank shall be supported in such manner that excessive concentrations of loads on the supporting portion of the shell are prevented.

7.3.6 In areas subject to earthquake, tank supports and connections shall be designed to resist damage as a result of such shocks.

7.4 Installation of Underground Tanks.

7.4.1 This section shall apply to tanks installed underground with backfill and to tanks buried beneath buildings.

7.4.2 Excavations for underground tanks shall be made in accordance with applicable building codes to avoid undermining the foundations of existing structures.

7.4.3 Underground tanks and tanks buried beneath buildings shall be located with respect to existing building foundations and supports so that the loads carried by the latter cannot be transmitted to the tank.

7.4.4 The distance from any part of an underground tank to the nearest wall of any basement or pit or to any property line shall not be less than 1 ft (0.3 m).

7.4.5* Underground tanks shall be installed in accordance with manufacturers' instructions and in accordance with applicable requirements of Chapter 23 of NFPA 30, *Flammable and Combustible Liquids Code*.

7.4.6 Underground tanks shall be equipped with vent opening(s) or automatically operated vent(s) for each tank compartment and interstitial space, which shall be arranged to discharge to the open air outside of buildings.

7.4.7* Underground tanks that are taken out of service shall be removed or permanently closed in accordance with the applicable requirements of NFPA 30, *Flammable and Combustible Liquids Code.*

7.5 Installation of Tanks Inside Buildings.

7.5.1 This section shall apply to tanks installed inside buildings, either enclosed or unenclosed, as herein described.

7.5.2 A safety can of less than 6.5 gal (26 L) capacity shall be permitted to be used for temporary fuel storage. It shall comply with UL 30, *Metal Safety Cans,* or UL 1313, *Nonmetallic Safety Cans for Petroleum Products,* and shall be specifically approved only for temporary use.

7.5.3 A supply tank of 60 gal (227 L) or less capacity shall be constructed in accordance with ANSI/UL 142, *Standard for Steel Aboveground Tanks for Flammable and Combustible Liquids,* and shall be specifically approved for permanent or temporary purposes.

7.5.4 A supply tank that exceeds 60 gal (227 L) capacity shall be installed on the lowest floor (story, cellar, or basement) of a building, except as provided for in 7.5.5.

7.5.5 A maximum of 660 gal (2500 L) of storage tank capacity shall be permitted to be installed on a higher floor, provided the following conditions are met:

(1) The higher floor does not have any floor or open space directly below it.
(2) The higher floor is provided with a liquidtight sill, containment device, or equivalent means having the ability to hold a minimum of 15 percent of the aggregate tank capacity to prevent spilled heating fuel from entering an adjacent, lower area.

7.5.6 A tank of less than 10 gal (38 L) capacity shall not be placed within 2 ft (0.6 m) from any ignition source, either in or external to the appliance being served, nor shall it be placed in a manner such that the temperature of the fuel in the tank exceeds the temperature of its surroundings by 25°F (14°C) or more.

7.5.7 A tank of capacity between 10 gal and 1320 gal (38 L and 5000 L) shall not be placed within 5 ft (1.5 m) horizontally from any open flame or fuel burning appliance unless separated from the source of heat by a barrier having a 1-hour fire resistance rating extending horizontally at least 1 ft (0.3 m) past the liquid fuel–burning appliance or the tank, whichever is greater, and extending vertically from floor to ceiling.

7.5.8 A tank of a capacity between 10 gal and 330 gal (38 L and 1250 L) that is provided with an opening in the bottom for use as a fuel supply connection to an appliance or as a drain shall be arranged as follows:

(1) The tank shall be pitched toward the opening with a slope of not less than ¼ in./ft (20 mm/m).
(2) Each supply line shall be provided with a readily accessible, thermally actuated automatic shutoff valve installed as close as practical to the tank. *(See also 8.7.3).*
(3) A properly sized and rated fuel filter or strainer shall be installed in the fuel supply line to the appliance downstream and within 6 in. (150 mm) of the thermally actuated automatic shutoff valve required by 7.5.8(2).
(4) Where three or more tanks are installed as part of a fuel storage system, each appliance supply line shall be provided with its own readily accessible safety shutoff valve.

7.5.9 Each tank or tank system shall be equipped with separate fill and vent openings.

7.5.10 Each tank shall be equipped with a gauging device. *(See 8.10.2.)*

7.5.11 Any unused opening in a tank shall be closed by a vaportight threaded plug or cap.

7.5.12 A tank or tank system shall be permitted to supply more than one liquid fuel–burning appliance.

7.5.13 Where a tank or tank system is not located in a dedicated room or enclosure, the maximum capacity in the building shall not exceed 1320 gal (5000 L) for a nonengineered system or 1375 gal (5200 L) for an engineered system, unless the installation meets the criteria in 7.5.13.1 or 7.5.13.2.

7.5.13.1 Fuel tanks of any size shall be permitted within a mechanical room, provided the room is designed using recognized engineering practices with suitable fire detection, fire suppression, and containment means to prevent the spread of fire beyond the room of origin.

7.5.13.2 Where a tank or tank system is not located in a dedicated room or enclosure, but is separated from other tank(s) by construction having a fire resistance rating of at least 2 hours, the maximum capacity in each separate area shall not exceed the quantities specified in 7.5.13. The maximum total capacity in the building shall not be limited.

7.5.13.3 Where a tank or tank system is located in a dedicated room or enclosure that is separated from the rest of the building by construction having a fire resistance rating of at least 1 hour, the maximum total capacity in the room shall not exceed 1320 gal (5000 L) for a nonengineered system or 1375 gal (5200 L) for an engineered system.

7.5.13.4 Where a tank or tank system is located in a dedicated room or enclosure that is separated from the rest of the building by construction having a fire resistance rating of at least 3 hours, the maximum total capacity in the room shall be permitted to exceed 1320 gal (5000 L) for a nonengineered system or 1375 gal (5200 L) for an engineered system.

7.5.13.5 Dedicated rooms or enclosures shall meet all applicable requirements of Section 7.6.

7.5.13.6 Tanks shall not obstruct quick and safe access to any utility service meters, electrical panelboards, or shutoff valves.

7.6 Requirements for Dedicated Tank Rooms and Tank Enclosures.

7.6.1 Each tank room or tank enclosure shall have a doorway with a noncombustible liquidtight sill or ramp at least 6 in. (150 mm) high and a self-closing, listed fire door that meets the requirements of NFPA 80, *Standard for Fire Doors and Other Opening Protectives.*

7.6.1.1 If the sill or ramp is more than 6 in. (150 mm) high, the walls of the room or enclosure shall be built to withstand the static head that would be expected in event of a fuel spill, up to the height corresponding to the expected spill depth.

7.6.2 Fire doors for rooms or enclosures of 2-hour fire-resistant construction shall have a fire protection rating of 1½ hours.

7.6.3 Fire doors for rooms or enclosures of 3-hour fire-resistant construction shall have a fire protection rating of at least 3 hours.

7.6.4 Each tank room or tank enclosure shall be provided with means to ventilate the room or enclosure prior to its being entered for inspection or repair.

7.6.5 A tank installed in a room or area having a fire resistance rating of 2 hours or less shall be of such size and shape that it can be installed in and removed from the room or area and from the building as a unit (i.e., in one piece).

7.7 Auxiliary Tanks.

7.7.1 Auxiliary tanks shall not exceed 60 gal (227 L) capacity and shall be used only for connection in the supply line between the main tank and the appliance.

7.7.2 Auxiliary tanks shall comply with 7.2.7.1(5).

7.7.3 Auxiliary tanks shall be filled by pump transfer through continuous piping from the supply tank.

7.7.4 Auxiliary tanks shall be located at a level above the top of the supply tank from which they are filled.

7.8 Installation of Outside Aboveground Tanks.

7.8.1 This section shall apply to tanks that are installed aboveground outside of buildings. This section shall not apply to a centralized oil distribution system.

7.8.2 A tank or tanks whose capacity does not exceed 660 gal (2500 L) shall be permitted to be installed outside of and adjacent to a building, provided they are separated from the nearest line of adjoining property by the following minimum distance:

(1) 5 ft (1.5 m) for tanks not exceeding 275 gal (1040 L) capacity
(2) 10 ft (3 m) for tanks greater than 275 gal (1040 L) capacity, but not exceeding 660 gal (2500 L) capacity

7.8.3 A tank or tanks whose capacity exceeds 660 gal (2500 L) shall be installed in accordance with all applicable requirements of Chapter 22 of NFPA 30, *Flammable and Combustible Liquids Code.*

7.8.4* Outside aboveground tanks and their appurtenances and supports shall be protected from external corrosion by a coating suitable for exterior use.

7.8.5 Tanks that are intended for temporary supply to an appliance shall comply with 7.2.7.1(5).

7.9 Tank Heating Systems.

7.9.1 Where tanks are provided with heating systems to maintain fuel at the required temperature for proper atomization, the heating systems shall meet the requirements of 7.9.2 through 7.9.4, as applicable.

7.9.2* Where tanks are heated by steam coils, the maximum operating pressure of the steam coils shall not exceed a gauge pressure of 15 psi (gauge pressure of 105 kPa).

7.9.2.1 Where a pressure-reducing valve is used to limit the steam pressure to a gauge pressure of 15 psi (gauge pressure of 105 kPa) or less, the following shall apply:

(1) A relief valve set at not more than a gauge pressure of 5 psi (gauge pressure of 35 kPa) above the normal pressure in the coil shall be provided.
(2) Provision shall be made to limit the steam temperature to 250°F (121°C).

7.9.3 Where tanks are heated by hot water coils, the hot water shall be provided by indirect heaters and the maximum temperature of the water shall be limited to 250°F (121°C).

7.9.4 Where tanks are heated by electric heaters, the heaters shall be equipped with listed and approved thermostats designed to prevent the fuel from exceeding its minimum flash point.

7.10 Special Storage Arrangements. In particular installations, the provisions of Chapter 7 shall be permitted to be altered by the authority having jurisdiction after consideration of special features such as the following:

(1) Topographical conditions, barricades, walls, and proximity to buildings or adjoining property
(2) Height and character of construction and nature of occupancies of such buildings
(3) Capacity and construction of proposed fuel tanks
(4) Characteristics and properties of the combustible liquid fuels to be stored
(5) Degree of private fire protection to be provided
(6) Capability of the fire department to cope with combustible liquid fires

7.11 Tank Leakage Testing and Periodic Inspection.

7.11.1 All shop-built and field-erected tanks shall be leak tested before they are placed in service in accordance with one of the following, as applicable:

(1) For shop-built tanks, the manufacturers' instructions
(2) For field-erected tanks, Section 21.5 of NFPA 30, *Flammable and Combustible Liquids Code*

Exception: The ASME code stamp or a listing mark acceptable to the authority having jurisdiction shall be evidence of compliance with this test.

7.11.2 Following completion of a new installation, the tank and its piping shall be inspected for leakage during the initial fill by a qualified technician and, if a leak is found, the tank or piping shall be repaired and retested.

7.11.3 Each tank shall be periodically inspected by a qualified technician for evidence of leakage and shall be maintained liquidtight. Tanks found to be leaking shall be repaired or replaced.

7.12 Abandonment and Removal from Service of Tanks and Related Equipment. If a tank and its related piping are abandoned for whatever reason, the tank and all piping connected to it, including the outside fill and vent piping and any piping connected to the appliance, shall be emptied of all contents, cleaned, removed from the premises or property, and disposed of in accordance with applicable local, state, and federal rules and regulations.

Exception: If a liquid fuel–burning appliance is converted to an alternate fuel, but the tank is kept in place so that it can be returned to service at some future date, the following requirements shall be met before the alternate fuel is used:

(1) The entire contents of the tank shall be completely removed and the tank purged of all vapors.
(2) The fuel tank vent line shall remain intact and open.
(3) The outside fill pipe shall be capped and filled with concrete, and all remaining piping, other than the vent line, shall be capped or sealed.

7.13 Fuel Storage Systems That Are Permanently Taken Out of Service.

7.13.1 If a fuel storage tank is permanently removed from service for whatever reason, the tank and all piping connected to it, including the outside fill and vent piping and any supply piping connected to the appliance, shall be:

(1) Emptied of all liquid contents and sludge
(2) Cleaned and rendered free of combustible vapors
(3) Removed from the premises or property
(4) Properly disposed of in accordance with all applicable local, state, and federal rules and regulations

7.13.2 The remover/installer of a tank taken out of service shall submit an affidavit of compliance to the authority having jurisdiction or to the tank owner stating that such fuel storage system was removed, in compliance with this section.

7.14 Permanent Abandonment of Underground Tanks. If an underground fuel storage tank is permanently removed from service, the requirements of 21.7.4.3.3 of NFPA 30, *Flammable and Combustible Liquids Code*, shall apply. (*See also Annex C of NFPA 30.*)

Chapter 8   Heating Fuel Piping Systems and Components

8.1 Scope. This chapter shall apply to piping systems and components used to provide filling and venting of tanks and transfer of heating fuel from tanks to heating fuel–burning appliances and equipment.

8.2 Acceptable Piping — Types and Materials.

8.2.1 Tank fill and vent piping shall be one of the types listed in 8.2.1.1 and 8.2.1.2, with male or female threaded ends that comply with a recognized thread specification.

8.2.1.1 For aboveground fill and vent piping, only the following types and materials shall be permitted:

(1) Minimum Schedule 40 steel pipe that complies with either ANSI/ASME B36.10M, *Standard on Welded and Seamless Wrought Steel Pipe*, ASTM A 53/53M, *Welded and Seamless Steel Pipe (Black & Galvanized)*; or ASTM A 106, *Seamless Carbon Steel Pipe (High Temp Service)*
(2) Minimum Schedule 40 brass pipe that complies with ASTM B 43, *Seamless Red Brass Pipe*
(3) Other piping that is part of an engineered fuel storage system that is listed, installed in accordance with manufacturer's instructions, and approved by the authority having jurisdiction

8.2.1.2 For underground fill and vent piping, only the following types and materials shall be permitted:

(1) Listed nonmetallic piping that complies with UL 971, *Underground Nonmetallic Piping for Flammable Liquids*
(2) Listed metallic piping that complies with SU 971A, *Underground Metallic Piping for Flammable Liquids*
(3) Steel pipe that meets 8.2.1.1(1)
(4) Brass pipe that meets 8.2.1.1(2)

8.2.2 Fuel supply lines shall be one of the piping types listed in 8.2.2.1 or 8.2.2.2, with threaded ends that comply with a recognized thread specification or tubing types intended for flared or engineered connections.

8.2.2.1 For aboveground fuel supply lines, only the following types and materials shall be permitted:

(1) Minimum Schedule 40 steel pipe that complies with ANSI/ASME B36.10M, *Welded and Seamless Wrought Steel Pipe*, ASTM A 53/53M, *Welded and Seamless Steel Pipe (Black & Galvanized)*; or ASTM A 106, *Seamless Carbon Steel Pipe (High Temp Service)*
(2) Minimum Schedule 40 brass pipe that complies with ASTM B 43, *Seamless Red Brass Pipe*
(3) Listed flexible metal pipe rated for aboveground use, where rigid connections are impractical
(4) Minimum 0.032 in. thick copper tubing that complies with ASTM B 75, *Seamless Copper Tube*, ASTM B 88, *Seamless Copper Water Tube*, or ASTM B 280, *Seamless Copper Tube for Air Conditioning & Refrigeration Service*
(5) Minimum 0.032 in. thick brass tubing that complies with ASTM B 135, *Seamless Brass Tube*
(6) Minimum 0.035 in. thick stainless steel tubing that complies with ASTM A 254, *Copper-Brazed Steel Tubing*; or ASTM A 269, *Seamless & Welded Stainless Steel Tubing*

8.2.2.2 For underground fuel supply lines, only the following types and materials shall be permitted:

(1) Listed nonmetallic piping that complies with UL 971, *Underground Nonmetallic Piping for Flammable Liquids*
(2) Listed corrosion resistant metallic piping that complies with SU 971A, *Underground Metallic Piping for Flammable Liquids*
(3) Listed corrosion resistant flexible metal piping rated for underground use, where rigid connections are impractical
(4) Corrosion-resistant copper tubing in accordance with 8.2.2.1(4), corrosion-resistant brass tubing in accordance with 8.2.2.1(5), or stainless steel tubing in accordance with 8.2.2.1(6)

8.2.2.2.1 Except where within 12 in. (300 mm) of a tank or appliance, tubing of copper, brass, or stainless steel, as identified in 8.2.2.2, shall be either provided with a listed corrosion-resistant coating or shall be installed through a corrosion-resistant conduit.

8.3 Acceptable Fittings — Types and Materials.

8.3.1 Pipe fittings shall be malleable iron, steel, stainless steel, or brass with male or female thread types that comply with a recognized thread specification. Threads shall be of the type, size, and direction that match with the pipe end threads with which they connect and shall be made liquidtight with suitable pipe joint or sealing compounds.

8.3.2 Tubing fittings shall be of listed types suitable for metal-to-metal flare or engineered connections for the metals and thicknesses of the tubing with which they connect. They shall be of the type and size that match with the tube end flare or engineered fitting with which they connect. They shall be flared or connected by use of the tools and methods recommended by the fitting manufacturer.

8.3.3 Other fittings and connection types shall be permitted if they are part of an engineered system that is listed for use with heating fuel and installed in accordance with the manufacturer's instructions.

8.3.4 Cast iron fittings shall not be used.

8.4 Piping System Design.

8.4.1 Piping systems shall be:

(1) Liquidtight
(2) Substantially supported
(3) Protected against physical damage

8.4.2 Proper allowance shall be made for expansion, contraction, jarring, and vibration of piping systems.

8.4.3 Piping systems made of combustible materials shall not be used inside of buildings or aboveground outside of buildings unless listed with at least a 30-minute fire rating.

8.4.4 Piping systems for underground tanks shall be provided with double swing joints or flexible connectors or shall be otherwise arranged to permit the tanks to settle without impairing the tightness of the piping system.

8.4.5 All connections to an underground tank shall be made through the top of the tank, except as provided for in 9.2.10.

8.4.6 Fuel shall not be transferred through piping to an appliance by pressurization of the tank.

8.4.7 Each tank or tank system shall be equipped with separate fill and vent pipes, both of which shall terminate aboveground outside the building.

8.5 Tank Fill Piping.

8.5.1 The fill pipe connected to the tank shall be large enough and so located as to permit ready filling in a manner that minimizes spills. The fill pipe shall also be:

(1) At least 1¼ in. (30 mm) nominal pipe size
(2) Pitched toward the tank
(3) Protected from physical damage
(4) Without sags or traps where liquid can collect

8.5.2 For tanks that directly supply a fuel-burning appliance and are intended to be filled by hose from a delivery vehicle, the fill pipe shall terminate as follows:

(1) Outside the building at a point at least 2 ft (0.6 m) from any building opening
(2) In a manner that prevents spills when the filling hose is disconnected

8.5.3 For tanks that directly supply a used oil–burning appliance and are intended to be filled either by hose from a delivery vehicle or by hand at the point of use, the fill pipe shall be permitted to terminate as follows:

(1) In accordance with NFPA 30A, *Code for Motor Fuel Dispensing Facilities and Repair Garages*
(2) With a funnel provided with a quarter-turn shutoff valve between the funnel and the tank

8.5.4 The end of the fill pipe shall be equipped with a tight metal cover designed to resist entry of water and shall be identified as a heating fuel fill opening.

8.6 Tank Vent Piping.

8.6.1 Vent piping connected to a tank shall be large enough and so located as to permit adequate normal fill and emergency venting. The vent pipe shall also be:

(1) Sized for the tank capacity in accordance with Table 7.2.5.1
(2) Pitched toward the tank
(3) Protected from physical damage
(4) Without sags or traps where liquid can collect
(5) Without obstructions other than an audible alarm at the tank opening

8.6.2 All vent pipes shall terminate outside of buildings at a point not less than 2 ft (0.6 m) from any building opening.

8.6.2.1 Vent pipes shall terminate high enough above the ground to avoid being obstructed by snow and ice.

8.6.2.2 Vent pipes shall terminate not more than 12 ft (3.6 m) from the fill pipe and at a point visible from the fill point.

8.6.3 The outer end of the vent pipe shall terminate in a corrosion-resistant weatherproof vent cap.

8.6.4 Vent caps shall have a minimum free open area equal to the cross-sectional area of the vent pipe and shall have screens No. 4 mesh or coarser.

8.7 Fuel Supply Piping and Return Piping.

8.7.1 The fuel supply piping between the supply tank and the appliance shall be:

(1) At least nominal ⅜ in. (10 mm) pipe or tubing
(2) Large enough to meet the fuel consumption rate of the appliance
(3) Provided with a shutoff valve at the outlet, for an aboveground tank
(4) Provided with a shutoff valve where an oil line enters a building, for an underground tank

8.7.2 The fuel supply piping from the supply tank shall be connected to the top of the tank, except for the following cases:

(1) Tanks of 330 gal (1250 L) or less
(2) Tanks with cross-connections

8.7.3 A readily accessible fusible link safety shutoff valve shall be installed:

(1) As close as practical to the burner(s) supply connection
(2) Immediately upstream of the filter and inside the building, if the piping passes through a foundation

8.7.4 The pressure at the fuel supply inlet to an appliance shall not exceed a gauge pressure of 3 psi (gauge pressure of 21 kPa), unless the appliance is approved for a higher inlet pressure.

8.7.5 Threaded pipe or valve ends installed in a tank bottom opening for gravity feed shall not penetrate above the bottom of the tank shell.

8.7.5.1 Use of stem pieces or other modifications to valves shall not circumvent the requirement of 8.7.5 to prevent water in the tank from draining out the bottom opening.

8.7.6 Unions or fittings that require gaskets or packings shall not be used in fuel lines.

8.7.7 Fuel Return Piping. A return line from a burner or a pump back to a supply tank shall have no valves or obstructions except for a hard-seat or ball valve with the handle removed and shall enter the top of the same tank.

8.8 Auxiliary Tank Piping.

8.8.1 An auxiliary tank shall be provided with an overflow pipe draining to the supply tank and extending into the top of the supply tank, unless the auxiliary tank is specifically listed for use without an overflow pipe.

8.8.2 An overflow pipe from an auxiliary tank shall have no valves or obstructions.

8.9 Piping for Cross-Connected Tanks.

8.9.1 Cross-connection of two tanks of not more than 660 gal (2500 L) aggregate capacity to the same fuel-burning appliance(s) shall be permitted if piped in accordance with Figure 8.9.1.

8.9.2 Cross-connection of three tanks of not more than 990 gal (3750 L) aggregate capacity to the same fuel-burning appliance(s) shall be permitted if piped in accordance with Figure 8.9.2.

8.9.3 Cross-connection of four tanks of not more than 1320 gal (5000 L) aggregate capacity to the same fuel-burning appliance(s) shall be permitted if piped in accordance with Figure 8.9.3.

8.9.4 Cross-connection of multiple tanks to the same burner or to the same group of burners using single fill and vent pipes shall be permitted in accordance with 8.9.1, 8.9.2, or 8.9.3, provided the tanks are rigidly secured to a common slab or foundation.

8.9.5 All fill and vent pipes shall drain toward the tank.

8.9.6 Vent pipes from more than one tank shall be permitted to be manifolded and connected into one outlet pipe.

8.9.6.1 The outlet pipe shall be at least one pipe size larger than the largest individual vent pipe connected thereto.

8.9.6.2 In no case shall the point of connection between two or more vent pipes be lower than the top of the fill pipe opening.

8.10 Pumps, Valves, Gauges, and Appurtenances.

8.10.1 Tanks, including each compartment of multi-compartment tanks, in which a constant fuel level is not maintained by an automatic pump shall be equipped with a method of determining the fuel level.

8.10.2 Gauging devices, such as liquid level indicators or signals, shall be designed and installed so that fuel or vapor will not be discharged into a building.

8.10.3 Supply tanks provided with fill and vent pipes shall be provided with a device to indicate either visually or audibly and within 12 ft (3.5 m) of the fill point, as specified by 8.6.2.2, when the fuel in the tank has reached a predetermined safe level.

Exception No. 1: Aboveground tanks that do not exceed 330 gal (1250 L) capacity shall rely on only an audible fill alarm to determine safe fill levels.

Exception No. 2: Underground tanks that can be filled with a fill pipe having an integral audible alarm that indicates a predetermined safe level.

8.10.4 Supply tanks shall not be equipped with a glass gauge.

8.10.5 An automatic pump that is not an integral part of a burner shall be listed and shall be installed in full compliance with its listing.

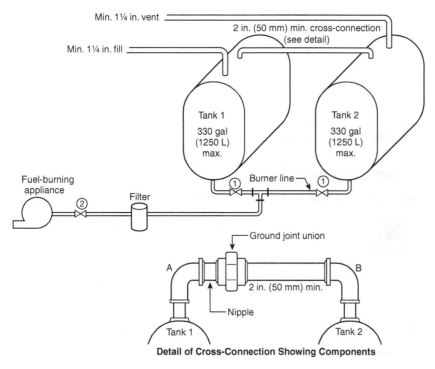

Notes:
① Fusible link safety shutoff valve required by 8.10.6(1).
② Fusible link safety shutoff valve required by 8.10.6(2).

For SI units, 1 gal = 3.785 L, 1 in. = 25 mm.

FIGURE 8.9.1   Cross-Connection of Two Fuel Tanks of Not More Than 660 gal (2500 L) Aggregate Capacity.

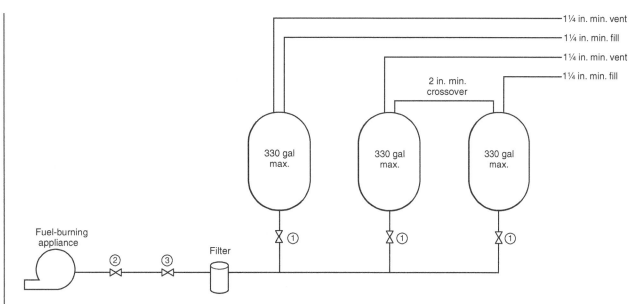

Notes:

① Fusible link safety shutoff valve required by 8.10.6(1).

② Fusible link safety shutoff valve required by 8.10.6(2).

③ Safety shutoff valve required by 7.5.8(4).

For SI units, 1 gal = 3.785 L, 1 in. = 25 mm.

FIGURE 8.9.2 Cross-Connection of Three Fuel Tanks of Not More Than 990 gal (3750 L) Aggregate Capacity.

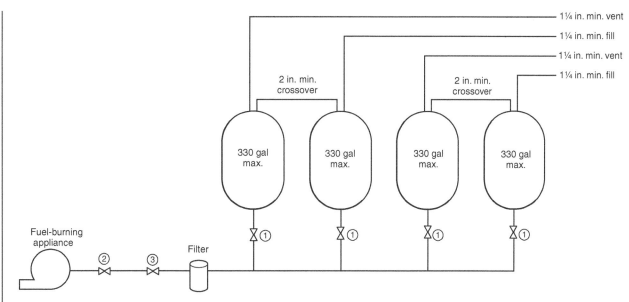

Notes:

① Fusible link safety shutoff valve required by 8.10.6(1).

② Fusible link safety shutoff valve required by 8.10.6(2).

③ Safety shutoff valve required by 7.5.8(4).

For SI units, 1 gal = 3.785 L, 1 in. = 25 mm.

FIGURE 8.9.3 Cross-Connection of Four Fuel Tanks of Not More Than 1320 gal (5000 L) Aggregate Capacity.

8.10.6 A readily accessible fusible link safety shutoff valve that closes against the supply pressure shall be installed at each of the following points:

(1) Within 6 in. (150 mm) of the filter on the tank side of the filter
(2) Within 12 in. (300 mm) of the inlet connection to the burner

8.10.7 Test wells shall be equipped with a tight-fitting metal cover.

8.11 Testing of Fuel Supply Piping.

8.11.1 Unless fuel supply piping and all fittings are visible for inspection, they shall be tested for leaks by either a pressure test method in accordance with 8.11.3 or a vacuum test method in accordance with 8.11.4 before being covered, enclosed, or placed into service.

8.11.2 Before oil supply lines are tested for leaks, any supply tank and any fuel-burning appliance shall be isolated from pressure, unless rated for the applicable test pressure or vacuum.

8.11.3 Pressure testing for leakage shall be conducted with air or an inert gas and shall be held for a time sufficient to conduct a complete visual inspection of all piping and fittings, but in no case for less than 10 minutes after stabilization.

8.11.3.1 A gauge pressure of at least 5.0 psi (35 kPa), but not more than 10 psi (70 kPa), shall be applied to all portions of the supply piping to be evaluated.

8.11.3.2 Leakage shall be detected by the appearance of bubbles after a soap-and-water solution or an equivalent leak detection fluid has been sprayed onto all joints.

8.11.4 Vacuum testing for leakage shall be conducted with a vacuum pump and vacuum gauge with 0.5 in. Hg (12 mm Hg) increments and accuracy of at least 2 percent. Vacuum shall be held for at least 30 minutes after stabilization with no loss.

8.11.4.1 A vacuum of at least 20 in. Hg (500 mm Hg) shall be applied to all portions of the supply piping to be evaluated.

8.11.4.2 Leakage shall be determined by any loss of vacuum after the test time.

8.11.5 Gauges used for leak testing shall be suitable for the test type, shall be in working order, and shall be calibrated. Gauges shall have a test range of not more than twice the test pressure and shall indicate in increments of not more than 1.0 psi (7 kPa) or 1.0 in. Hg (25 mm Hg).

Chapter 9   Oil Distribution Systems

9.1 Scope. This chapter shall apply to centralized oil distribution systems, as defined in 3.3.8, and to oil distribution systems for roof-mounted and ceiling-suspended oil-burning appliances.

9.2 Centralized Oil Distribution Systems.

9.2.1 A centralized oil distribution system shall meet the requirements of this section and all other applicable provisions of this standard.

9.2.2 The installation and maintenance of a centralized oil distribution system shall be supervised by a qualified person.

9.2.3 Plans showing the relative location of tanks, pumps, valves, piping, and structures to be supplied by the system shall be approved by and filed with the authority having jurisdiction.

9.2.4 Oil shall be permitted to be fed from the supply tank or tanks by gravity or by transfer pump.

9.2.5 All distribution piping outside of diked areas shall be underground.

9.2.6 The capacity of a single aboveground tank or the aggregate capacity of two or more aboveground tanks supplying a centralized oil distribution system shall not exceed 20,000 gal (75,700 L) nominal capacity.

9.2.7 Underground tanks installed in accordance with Section 7.4 shall be permitted to be of any capacity.

9.2.8 Tanks that supply a centralized oil distribution system shall meet all applicable requirements of Chapter 7.

9.2.9 Aboveground tanks shall be provided with spill control by means of diking meeting the requirements of NFPA 30, *Flammable and Combustible Liquids Code.*

9.2.10 The main distribution pipeline shall be permitted to be connected to a tank or tanks having an aggregate capacity not exceeding 20,000 gal (75,700 L) at a point below the liquid level.

9.2.10.1 Where this piping is so connected, a readily accessible internal or external shutoff valve shall be installed in the piping as close as practicable to the tank.

9.2.10.2 If external and aboveground, the shutoff valve and its tank connections shall be made of steel.

9.2.10.3 Connections between the tank(s) and the main pipeline shall be made with double swing joints or flexible connectors, or shall otherwise be arranged to permit the tank(s) to settle without damaging the system.

9.2.10.4 If located aboveground, the connections specified in 9.2.10.3 shall be located within the diked area.

9.2.11 A readily accessible and identified manual shutoff valve shall be installed either inside or outside of the structure in each branch supply pipeline that enters a building, mobile home, travel trailer, or other structure.

9.2.11.1 If inside, the valve shall be located directly adjacent to the point at which the supply line enters the structure.

9.2.11.2 If outside, the valve shall be protected from weather and damage.

9.2.12 A device shall be provided in the supply line at or ahead of the point where it enters the interior of the structure that will automatically shut off the oil supply, if the supply line between this device and the appliance is broken.

9.2.12.1 This device shall be located on the appliance side of the manual shutoff valve required in 9.2.11 and shall be solidly supported and protected from damage.

9.2.13 Means shall be provided to limit the oil pressure at the appliance inlet to a maximum gauge pressure of 3 psi (gauge pressure of 21 kPa).

9.2.13.1 If a pressure-reducing valve is used, it shall be a type approved for the service.

9.2.14 A device shall be provided that will automatically shut off the oil supply to the appliance if the oil pressure at the appliance inlet exceeds a gauge pressure of 8 psi (gauge pressure of 55 kPa). The device shall not be required under either of the following conditions:

(1) Where the distribution system is supplied from a gravity tank and the maximum hydrostatic head of oil in the tank is such that the oil pressure at the appliance inlet will not exceed a gauge pressure of 8 psi (gauge pressure of 55 kPa)
(2) Where a means is provided to automatically shut off the oil supply if the pressure-regulating device provided in accordance with 9.2.13 fails to regulate the pressure as required

9.2.15 Only appliances equipped with primary safety controls specifically listed for the appliance shall be connected to a centralized oil distribution system.

9.2.16 Accurate inventory records shall be maintained and reconciled on all storage tanks for indication of leakage from tanks or piping.

9.3 Oil Distribution Systems for Roof-Mounted or Ceiling-Suspended Oil-Fired Units.

9.3.1 An oil distribution system for roof-mounted or ceiling-suspended oil-burning appliances shall meet the requirements of this section and all other applicable provisions of this standard.

9.3.2 The installation and maintenance of the oil distribution system shall be supervised by a qualified person.

9.3.3 Plans showing the relative location of tanks, pumps, valves, piping, and their relationship to structures supplied by the systems shall be approved by and filed with the authority having jurisdiction.

9.3.4 Oil shall be permitted to be fed to the burner(s) directly from a storage tank or by means of a fuel distribution system that includes a transfer pump.

9.3.4.1 Where fed directly from a storage tank, the fuel supply system shall be designed so that the burner fuel unit operates with less than 10 in. Hg (34 kPa) vacuum at the inlet under normal operating conditions.

9.3.4.2 If the requirements of 9.3.4.1 cannot be met, a fuel supply system incorporating a transfer pump(s) shall be provided.

9.3.5 The fuel supply system shall meet the following requirements:

(1) All components (pumps, reservoirs, valves, regulators, relief valves, controls, and so forth) shall be listed for use with fuel oil.
(2) Control and relief provisions shall be provided to prevent pressurizing the main distribution pipelines to any point more than 50 percent above the normal working pressure.
(3) Dead-ended main distribution pipelines shall not be permitted unless provisions are made for air purging, and the purge points shall be closed by plugs or caps when not actually in use.
(4) Means shall be provided to limit the oil pressure at the burner inlet to a maximum gauge pressure of 3 psi (gauge pressure of 21 kPa).
(5) If a pressure-reducing valve is to be used, it shall be a type approved for the service.

9.3.6 The capacity of a single aboveground tank or the aggregate capacity of two or more aboveground tanks shall not exceed 20,000 gal (75,700 L) nominal capacity.

9.3.7 Underground tanks installed in accordance with Section 7.4 shall be permitted to be of any capacity.

9.3.8 Tanks, piping, pumps, and valves shall meet all applicable requirements of Chapters 7 and 8.

9.3.9 If required by design, individual supply tanks, including auxiliary tanks, connected to burners shall meet the requirements of 7.5.4, 7.7.4, and Section 8.8.

9.3.10 Valves and drip trays (roof-mounted units only) shall be provided to prevent oil spills during servicing.

9.3.11 A readily accessible and identified manual shutoff valve shall be installed in each branch supply pipeline that serves an individual burner and in the oil distribution line.

9.3.11.1 This valve shall be permitted to be either inside or outside of a protective enclosure.

9.3.11.2 If inside, the valve shall be located directly adjacent to the point at which the supply line enters the protective enclosure.

9.3.11.3 If outside, the valve shall be protected from weather and damage.

9.3.12 Only roof-mounted or ceiling-suspended appliances equipped with primary safety controls specifically listed for the appliance shall be connected to the distribution system.

9.3.13 A switch shall be provided in the electrical supply to the transfer pump.

9.3.13.1 The switch shall be permitted to be locked in the open position and shall be located at a convenient location so the fuel supply system can be shut down for maintenance.

9.3.13.2 Provisions shall be made so that shutdown of the fuel supply system interrupts the electrical supply to the appliances to which the fuel supply is connected. (*See also 10.5.9.*)

Chapter 10 Installation of Oil Burners and Oil-Burning Appliances

10.1 Scope. This chapter shall apply to installation of oil burners and oil-burning appliances and equipment.

10.2 Basic Requirements.

10.2.1 Installation of oil-burning boilers with inputs of 12,500,000 Btu/hr (3663 kW) and above shall meet the applicable requirements of NFPA 85, *Boiler and Combustion Systems Hazards Code.*

10.2.2 Installation of oil-burning ovens and furnaces within the scope of NFPA 86, *Standard for Ovens and Furnaces*, shall meet the applicable requirements of that standard.

10.2.3 Oil burners shall be permitted to be installed in boilers and furnaces.

10.2.4 Oil burners shall be permitted by the authority having jurisdiction for use in firing ovens, water heaters, ranges, special furnaces, and the like.

10.2.5 Where oil burners are installed in appliances originally designed for solid fuel, the ash door of the appliance shall be removed or bottom ventilation shall be provided to prevent the accumulation of vapors in the ash pit.

Exception: Where the ash pit is used as part of the combustion chamber.

10.2.6 Oil-burning appliances shall be installed in rooms that are large compared with the size of the appliance.

Exception: An appliance specifically listed for installation in a confined space, such as an alcove or closet, shall be permitted to be so installed when the installation complies with its listing.

10.2.7 In installations in confined spaces, the clearances from the appliance to the walls and ceilings shall not be less than those specified in the listing, regardless of the type of construction.

10.2.8 The oil-burning appliance shall have a suitable combustion chamber of firebrick, stainless steel, or other material, either furnished by the manufacturer or specified in the manufacturers' installation instructions.

10.2.9 Prior to installation of an oil burner, the furnace, boiler, or appliance into which it is installed shall be examined and shown to be in good condition. The combustion chamber and flue gas passages shall be examined and shown to be tight against leaks.

10.3 Posting of Instructions. Complete instructions for the care and operation of the appliance, as furnished by the manufacturer, shall be conspicuously posted near the appliance.

10.4 Replacement of Appliances and Chimneys. (Reserved)

10.5 Operating Controls.

10.5.1* Oil burners, other than oil stoves with integral tanks, shall be provided with some means for manually stopping the flow of oil to the burner.

10.5.1.1 Such device or devices shall be placed in a readily accessible location at a safe distance from the burner.

10.5.1.2 For electrically powered appliances, the requirement of 10.5.1 shall be accomplished by an identified switch in the burner supply circuit, placed outside of and adjacent to the entrance to the room where the appliance is located.

10.5.1.3 For appliances that are not electrically powered, an identifiable valve in the oil supply line, operable from a location that can be reached without passing near the burner, shall be used.

10.5.2 An electrical service disconnect switch, arranged to stop and start the oil burner, shall be installed at the appliance and shall be located so that it is within easy reach of the service technician for control of the oil burner while observing the flame.

10.5.3* Oil burners shall be equipped with a listed primary safety control of a type appropriate for the burner.

10.5.4* Each oil-burning appliance shall be provided with automatic limit controls that will prevent unsafe pressure or low water in a steam boiler, low water or over-temperature in a water boiler, or over-temperature in a furnace or heater.

10.5.5* Limiting controls and low-water shutoffs intended to prevent unsafe operation of heating equipment by opening an electrical circuit to the burner or oil shutoff device shall be so arranged as to effect the direct opening of that circuit, whether the switching mechanism is integral with the sensing element or remote from same.

Exception: A limit control that interrupts the pilot circuit of a magnetic-type motor controller, which, in turn, directly opens the safety circuit when it is necessary to interrupt a single-phase circuit carrying a load greater than the capacity of available limit controls or to interrupt a multiphase circuit, is acceptable.

10.5.6 A water heater shall be provided with water pressure, temperature, and vacuum-relief devices.

10.5.7 Means shall be provided to prevent siphoning in any boiler or tank with a circulating water heater attached.

10.5.8 Electric motor–driven oil burners with integral oil pumps and electric motor–driven pump sets for use with burners not equipped with integral pumps shall be provided with a motor controller that incorporates no-voltage protection and is wired into the power supply to the motor.

10.5.9 In systems where either steam or air is used for atomizing the fuel oil or where air for combustion is supplied by a source that can be interrupted without shutting off the oil supply, the fuel oil supply and the steam or air supply shall be interlocked so that the fuel oil supply is shut off immediately upon failure of the steam or air supply.

10.5.10 Where automatically operated oil burners are used in installations equipped with forced- or induced-draft fans, or both, means shall be provided to shut off the oil supply immediately upon fan failure.

10.5.11 Oil burners not equipped to provide safe automatic restarting after shutdown shall require manual restarting after any control functions to extinguish the burner flame.

10.5.12 An acceptance test of the primary safety control shall be conducted on any appliance where more than one burner is fired in a single combustion chamber or where one burner is adapted to fire in two or more combustion chambers.

10.5.12.1 The test shall ensure that the primary safety control will function properly in the event of ignition failure or unsafe flame extinguishment at any of the burners.

10.6 Specific Requirements for Installation of Boilers, Furnaces, Floor-Mounted Unit Heaters, and Water Heaters.

10.6.1 Appliances shall be installed with clearances from combustible material not less than those indicated in Figure 10.6.1 and Table 10.6.1.

Exception: Appliances specifically listed for installation with lesser clearances shall be permitted to be installed in accordance with their listing.

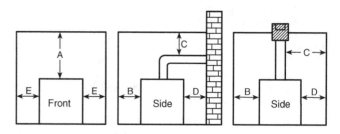

FIGURE 10.6.1 Clearances to Combustible Materials.

Table 10.6.1 Clearances to Combustible Material[1]

Classification as to Type of Appliance	Clearances (in.)						
	A Above[2]	Duct[3]	B Front	C Chimney[4] Connector	D Rear	Ec Casing Sides[5]	Ep Furnace Plenum Sides[6]
Form I	2[9]	2	24	18	6	6	2 or 6[10]
Form IA	6	—	24	18	6	6	—
Form II[7]	6	2	24	18	6	6	2
Form III[8]	18	18	48	18	18	18	18
Form IV	48	—	96	36	36	36	—
Form V	6	—	24	18	18	18	—

For SI units, 1 in. = 25 mm.

Notes:

(1) For multiple-fueled appliances that can fire solid fuels, see NFPA 211, *Standard for Chimneys, Fireplaces, Vents, and Solid Fuel-Burning Appliances*, and NFPA 90B, *Standard for the Installation of Warm Air Heating and Air-Conditioning Systems*.

(2) This column indicates clearances above the top of the appliance casing or above the top of the furnace bonnet or plenum.

(3) This column indicates clearance from a horizontal run of warm-air duct within 3 ft (900 mm) of upflow, downflow, or horizontal type warm-air furnaces.

(4) See Section 6.5 for installation of chimney connectors.

(5) This column indicates clearances from the sides of the appliance casing.

(6) This column is applicable only to a warm-air furnace provided with an external plenum for connection to duct systems and indicates clearances from all sides of the outlet air plenum.

(7) The clearance from the bottom of a suspended (horizontal) furnace that is not otherwise classified as a low-heat industrial appliance shall not be less than 6 in. (150 mm).

(8) The clearance to combustible material from the bottom of a suspended (horizontal) furnace that is not classified as a low-heat industrial appliance under Form III, from a suspended-type unit heater that is classified under Form V, or from a unit heater that is classified as a low-heat industrial appliance under Form III shall not be less than 18 in. (450 mm).

(9) This clearance shall be permitted to be reduced to 1 in. (25 mm) for a listed, forced-air or gravity system equipped with a limit control that cannot be set higher than 200°F (93°C).

(10) Clearance is 2 in. (50 mm) for upflow warm-air furnaces and 6 in. (150 mm) for downflow warm-air furnaces.

Description of Classifications for Use with Table 10.6.1

Form I. Automatically fired upflow- or downflow-type warm-air furnaces, excluding horizontal types not larger than 100 ft³ (2.8 m³) in size (excluding blower compartments and burner equipment).

Form IA. Floor-mounted unit heaters, not larger than 100 ft³ (2.8 m³) in size, excluding blower or fan compartment and burner.

Form II. Horizontal-type warm-air furnaces; water wall-type boilers operating at not more than 250°F (121°C) for water boilers and at not more than 15 psig (gauge pressure of 103 kPa) pressure for steam boilers; water heaters not larger than 100 ft³ (2.8 m³) in size (excluding burner equipment and blower compartments of furnaces).

Form III. Low-heat industrial appliances; floor-mounted-type and suspended-type warm-air furnaces not classified under Forms I and II; steam boilers operating at not more than a gauge pressure of 50 psi (gauge pressure of 345 kPa) pressure and not classified under Form II; water boilers operating at a water temperature not more than the temperature of saturated steam at not more than a gauge pressure of 50 psi pressure and not classified under Form II; unit heaters not classified under Forms IA or V.

Form IV. Medium-heat industrial appliances; steam boilers operating at a gauge pressure of over 50 psi pressure.

Form V. Suspended-type unit heaters not more than 100 ft³ (2.8 m³) in size (excluding fan compartment and burner equipment).

10.6.1.1 In no case shall the clearances used interfere with providing combustion air or providing access to the appliance. *(See Chapters 4 and 5.)*

10.6.1.2 Chimney connectors shall be installed in accordance with Section 6.5.

10.6.1.3 When multiple-fueled appliances using solid fuels are installed, the clearances and mounting requirements of NFPA 211, *Standard for Chimneys, Fireplaces, Vents, and Solid Fuel–Burning Appliances*, shall apply.

10.6.2 Appliances shall be permitted to be installed in rooms, but not in alcoves or closets, with lesser clearances to combustible material, provided the combustible material or appliance is protected as described in Table 10.6.2 and Figure 10.6.2(a), Figure 10.6.2(b), and Figure 10.6.2(c).

Table 10.6.2 Reduction of Clearances with Specified Forms of Protection

	Allowable Clearance with Specified Protection (in.)									
	Where the required clearance with no protection from the appliance or chimney connector is:									
	36 in.		18 in.		12 in.		9 in.		6 in.	
Type of Protection[1]	Above	Sides and Rear	Above	Sides and Rear	Above	Sides and Rear	Above	Sides and Rear	Above	Sides and Rear
(a) 3½ in. thick masonry wall without ventilated air space	—	24	—	12	—	9	—	6	—	5
(b) ½ in. insulation board over 1 in. glass fiber or mineral wool batts	24	18	12	9	9	6	6	5	4	3
(c) 0.024 in. (24-gauge) sheet metal over 1 in. glass fiber or mineral wool batts reinforced with wire on rear face with ventilated air space	18	12	9	6	6	4	5	3	3	3
(d) 3½ in. thick masonry wall with ventilated air space	—	12	—	6	—	6	—	6	—	6
(e) 0.024 in. (24-gauge) sheet metal with ventilated air space	18	12	9	6	6	4	5	3	3	2
(f) ½ in. thick insulation board with ventilated air space	18	12	9	6	6	4	5	3	3	3
(g) 0.024 in. (24-gauge) sheet metal with ventilated air space over 0.024 in. (24-gauge) sheet metal with ventilated air space	18	12	9	6	6	4	5	3	3	3
(h) 1 in. glass fiber or mineral wool batts sandwiched between 2 sheets 0.024 in. (24-gauge) sheet metal with ventilated air space	18	12	9	6	6	4	5	3	3	3

For SI units, 1 in. = 25 mm.

Notes:

(1) The type of protection specified is applied to and covers all surfaces of combustible material within the distance specified as the required clearance with no protection. [See Figure 10.6.2(a), Figure 10.6.2(b), and Figure 10.6.2(c) for additional information.]

(2) Reduction of clearances from combustible materials cannot interfere with combustion air, draft regulators, or accessibility for servicing.

(3) All clearances are measured from the outer surface of the combustible material to the nearest point on the surface of the appliance or connector, disregarding any intervening protection applied to the combustible material.

(4) Spacers and ties are of noncombustible material. No spacer or tie can be used directly opposite an appliance or connector.

(5) With all clearance reduction systems using ventilated air space, adequate provision for air circulation is to be provided as described. [See Figure 10.6.2(a) and Figure 10.6.2(b).]

(6) Provide at least 1 in. (25 mm) clearance between the reduction system and combustible walls and ceilings for reduction systems using ventilated air space.

(7) If a wall protector is mounted on a single flat wall away from corners, adequate air circulation can be provided by leaving only the bottom and top edges, or only the side and top edges open, with at least a 1 in. (25 mm) air gap.

(8) Mineral wool batts (blanket or board) are to have a minimum density of 8 lb/ft³ (128 kg/m³) and a minimum melting point of 1500°F (816°C).

(9) Insulation material used as part of a clearance reduction system is to have a thermal conductivity of 1 (Btu/in.)/(ft²/hr·°F) or less.

(10) Provide at least 1 in. (25 mm) between the appliance or connector and the protector. In no case is the clearance between the appliance or connector and the combustible material to be reduced below that allowed in the table.

(11) All clearances and thicknesses are minimum. Larger clearances and thicknesses are acceptable.

10.6.3 Floor-mounted appliances shall be placed in one the following ways:

(1) On floors of fire-resistive construction with noncombustible flooring or surface finish and with no combustible material against the underside thereof
(2) On fire-resistive slabs or arches having no combustible material against the underside thereof
(3) In accordance with their listing, if listed specifically for installation on a floor constructed of combustible material

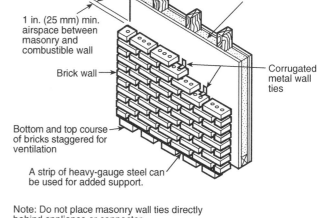

Note: Do not place masonry wall ties directly behind appliance or connector.

Masonry clearance reduction system

Masonry wall tie

FIGURE 10.6.2(b)   Masonry Clearance Reduction System.

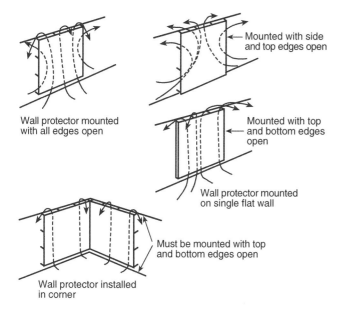

Wall protector mounted with all edges open

Mounted with side and top edges open

Mounted with top and bottom edges open

Wall protector mounted on single flat wall

Wall protector installed in corner

Must be mounted with top and bottom edges open

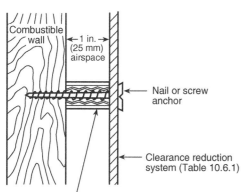

Note: 1 in. (25 mm) noncombustible spacer such as stacked washers, small-diameter pipe, tubing, or electrical conduit.

Masonry walls can be attached to combustible walls using wall ties.

Do not use spacers directly behind appliance or connector.

FIGURE 10.6.2(a)   Wall Protector Clearance Reduction System.

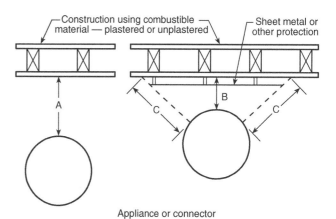

Appliance or connector

"A" equals the required clearance with no protection, as specified in Table 10.6.1.

"B" equals the reduced clearance permitted. The protection applied to combustible materials is required to extend far enough in each direction to make "C" equal "A." Plastered constructions having combustible supports are classed as combustible regardless of the type of lath.

FIGURE 10.6.2(c)   Extent of Protection Necessary to Reduce Clearances from Appliances or Chimney Connectors.

10.6.3.1* Such construction shall extend not less than 12 in. (0.3 m) beyond the appliance on all sides.

Exception No. 1: Appliances shall be permitted to be placed on combustible floors although not listed for such installation, provided the floor under the appliance is protected in accordance with the requirements of accepted building code practice.

Exception No. 2: An appliance listed for installation under Form I or II in Table 10.6.1 shall be permitted to be placed on a combustible floor that is protected with hollow masonry not less than 4 in. (100 mm) thick covered with sheet metal not less than 24 gauge, as shown in Figure 10.6.3.1. Such masonry shall be laid with ends unsealed and joints matched in such a way as to permit free circulation of air from side to side through the masonry. For such installations, the furnace shall be securely anchored to maintain the clearances required in Table 10.6.1.

10.6.4 The supply and return duct system of a central heating appliance shall be installed in accordance with NFPA 90A, *Standard for the Installation of Air-Conditioning and Ventilating Systems,* or NFPA 90B, *Standard for the Installation of Warm Air Heating and Air-Conditioning Systems,* whichever is applicable.

10.6.5 A return system shall be arranged so that negative pressure from the circulating fan cannot affect the air supply for combustion or act to draw products of combustion from joints or openings in the appliance, chimney connectors, or chimney.

10.6.6 A down-flow furnace shall be installed so that there are no open passages in the floor through which flame or hot

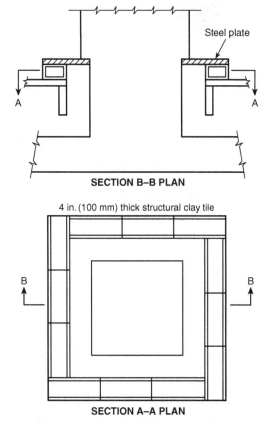

SECTION B–B PLAN

4 in. (100 mm) thick structural clay tile

SECTION A–A PLAN

FIGURE 10.6.3.1 Installation of Down-Flow Furnace on Combustible Floor.

gases from a fire originating in the room below the floor can travel to the room above.

10.6.7 A down-flow furnace shall be automatically operated and equipped with an approved temperature limit control that will limit outlet air temperature to 200°F (93°C). The furnace shall be designed to prevent unsafe temperatures in the event of reverse flow.

10.7 Specific Requirements for Attic Furnaces. A furnace installed in an attic shall be listed for such installation and installed in accordance with its listing.

10.8 Specific Requirements for Duct Furnaces.

10.8.1 A duct furnace shall be installed with clearances of at least 6 in. (150 mm) to adjacent walls, ceilings, and floors of combustible material, unless listed for installation at lesser clearance and installed in accordance with its listing.

10.8.2 A duct furnace and its chimney connector shall be permitted to be installed in a room, but not in a confined space such as an alcove or closet, with reduced clearances to combustible material, provided the combustible material is protected as described in Table 10.6.2 and Figure 10.6.2(a), Figure 10.6.2(b), and Figure 10.6.2(c) and the requirements for combustion air and accessibility comply with Chapters 4 and 5.

10.8.3 A duct furnace flue pipe shall be installed to provide a clearance to combustible material of not less than 18 in. (450 mm).

10.8.4 A duct furnace shall be firmly supported.

10.8.5 Access panels shall be provided in the ducts on both the upstream and downstream sides of the furnace.

10.8.6 Controls shall be located outside the duct except for the sensing element of a control.

10.9 Specific Requirements for Floor Furnaces.

10.9.1 Floor furnaces shall not be installed in floors of combustible construction unless specifically listed for such installation and installed in accordance with their listing. *(See Figure 10.6.3.1.)*

10.9.2 The floor around the furnace shall be braced and headed with a framework of material not lighter than the floor joists.

10.9.3 Floor furnaces shall be supported independently of the floor grilles.

10.9.4 A floor furnace shall be placed not closer than 6 in. (150 mm) to the nearest wall and shall be so placed that a door, drapery, or similar object cannot be nearer than 12 in. (300 mm) to any portion of the register of the furnace.

10.9.5 Wall-register models shall be placed not closer than 6 in. (150 mm) to a corner.

10.9.6 The bottom of a floor furnace shall have at least 6 in. (150 mm) clearance from the ground.

10.9.6.1 Where the ground must be excavated to provide this clearance, the excavation shall extend at least 12 in. (300 mm) beyond the furnace on all sides and at least 18 in. (450 mm) on the control side.

10.9.6.2 Where the excavation exceeds 12 in. (300 mm) or where the ground contour or moisture condition is such that water seepage is likely, a watertight pan constructed of copper, galvanized iron, or other suitable corrosion-resistant material, properly anchored in place, or a waterproof concrete pit, shall be provided under the furnace. The sides of the pan or pit shall extend 4 in. (100 mm) above ground level.

10.9.7 Floor furnaces shall be made accessible.

10.9.7.1 Openings in foundation walls and trap doors in floors shall not be smaller than 18 in. × 24 in. (450 mm × 600 mm) in dimension.

10.9.7.2 Underfloor passageways to the furnace shall not be smaller than 24 in. × 24 in. (600 mm × 600 mm).

10.9.8 Provision shall be made for proper air supply for combustion.

10.9.9 Listed floor furnaces shall be permitted to be installed in an upper floor of a building, provided the furnace assembly projects below into a utility room, closet, garage, or similar nonhabitable space.

10.9.9.1 In such installations, the floor furnace shall be completely enclosed (entirely separated from the nonhabitable space), with means for air intake and with access facilities for servicing on the control side.

10.9.9.2 The minimum furnace clearances shall be 6 in. (150 mm) to all sides and bottom.

10.9.9.3 The enclosure shall be constructed of Portland cement plaster on metal lath or material of equal fire resistance.

10.9.10 A floor furnace shall not be installed in the floor of any aisle or passageway of an auditorium, public hall, or public assembly room or in an exitway from any such room or space.

10.9.11 A floor furnace chimney connector shall be installed with not less than 9 in. (225 mm) clearances to combustible material, unless the combustible material is protected as described in Table 10.6.2 and in Figure 10.6.2(a), Figure 10.6.2(b), and Figure 10.6.2(c).

10.10 Specific Requirements for Furnaces Used with Refrigeration Systems.

10.10.1 A furnace shall not be installed in conjunction with a refrigeration coil where circulation of cooled air is provided by the blower unless the blower has sufficient capacity to overcome the external static resistance imposed by the duct system, furnace, and cooling coil at the airflow required for heating or cooling, whichever is greater.

10.10.2 To avoid condensation within heating elements, furnaces used in conjunction with cooling equipment shall be installed in parallel with or on the upstream side of cooling coils unless the furnace has been specifically listed for downstream installation.

10.10.3 With a parallel flow arrangement, the dampers or other means used to control the flow of air shall be sufficiently tight to prevent any circulation of cooled air through the unit.

10.10.4 Where furnaces are to be located upstream from cooling units, the cooling units shall be designed or equipped so that excessive temperatures or pressures are not developed.

10.10.5 Furnaces shall be permitted to be installed downstream from evaporative coolers or air washers if the heating element is made of corrosion-resistant material.

10.10.5.1 Stainless steel, ceramic-coated steel, or an aluminum-coated steel in which the bond between the steel and the aluminum is an iron-aluminum alloy shall be considered corrosion-resistant.

10.10.5.2 Air washers operating with chilled water, which deliver air below the dew point of the ambient air at the appliance, shall be considered refrigeration systems.

10.11 Specific Requirements for Industrial Furnaces and Boilers — Stationary Type.

10.11.1 Stationary-type industrial furnaces and power boilers shall include low-heat, medium-heat, and high-heat appliances. *(See Chapter 3, Definitions, for examples of each type.)*

10.11.2 Low-Heat Appliances.

10.11.2.1 Low-heat appliances shall be installed with clearances not less than those specified by Form III in Table 10.6.1.

10.11.2.1.1 Low-heat appliances that are approved for installation with lesser clearances than specified in 10.11.2.1 shall be permitted to be installed in accordance with their listing.

10.11.2.1.2 Low-heat appliances shall be permitted to be installed with lesser clearances to combustible material, provided the combustible material is protected as specified in Table 10.6.2 and Figure 10.6.2(a), Figure 10.6.2(b), and Figure 10.6.2(c).

10.11.2.2 Floor-mounted low-heat appliances shall be installed in one of the following ways:

(1) On the ground
(2) On floors of fire-resistive construction with noncombustible flooring or surface finish and with no combustible material against the underside thereof
(3) On fire-resistive slabs or arches having no combustible material against the underside thereof

10.11.2.2.1 The construction described in 10.11.2.2(2) and 10.11.2.2(3) shall extend not less than 12 in. (0.3 m) beyond the appliance on all sides.

10.11.2.2.2 Appliances that are listed specifically for installation on a floor constructed of combustible material shall be permitted to be placed in accordance with the conditions of their listing.

10.11.2.2.3 Low-heat appliances shall be permitted to be placed on combustible floors although not listed for such installation, provided the floor under the appliance is protected in accordance with the requirements of accepted building code practice.

10.11.3 Medium-Heat Appliances.

10.11.3.1 Medium-heat appliances shall be installed with clearances not less than those indicated by Form IV in Table 10.6.1.

10.11.3.2 Medium-heat appliances shall be installed in one of the following ways:

(1) On the ground
(2) On floors of fire-resistive construction with noncombustible flooring or surface finish and with no combustible material against the underside thereof
(3) On fire-resistive slabs or arches having no combustible material against the underside thereof

10.11.3.2.1 The construction described in 10.11.3.2(2) and 10.11.3.2(3) shall extend not less than 3 ft (900 mm) beyond the appliance on all sides.

10.11.3.2.2 Medium-heat appliances shall be permitted to be placed on combustible floors although not listed for such installation, provided the floor under the appliance is protected in accordance with accepted building code practice.

10.11.3.3 Rooms containing medium-heat appliances shall be provided with ventilation to prevent accumulation of hot air over or near the appliance.

10.11.4 High-Heat Appliances.

10.11.4.1 High-heat appliances shall be installed with clearances to combustible material of not less than 10 ft (3 m) at the sides and rear, not less than 15 ft (4.5 m) above, and not less than 30 ft (9 m) at the front or side where hot products are removed.

10.11.4.2 Rooms containing high-heat appliances shall be provided with ventilation to prevent accumulation of hot air over or near the appliance.

10.11.4.3 High-heat appliances shall be placed in either of the following ways:

(1) On the ground
(2) On floors of fire-resistive construction with noncombustible flooring or surface finish and with no combustible material against the underside thereof, with floors extending at least 10 ft (3 m) on all sides and at least 30 ft (9 m) at the front or side where hot products are removed

10.12 Specific Requirements for Miscellaneous Heaters (Air Heaters, Salamanders, and so forth).

10.12.1 A direct-fired heater or salamander shall not be used in an enclosed space or in proximity to combustible material.

10.12.2 A direct-fired heater or salamander shall be permitted to be used where salamanders fired by coal or coke are allowed.

10.12.3 An air heater shall be of a type designed to discharge air at a temperature not exceeding 250°F (121°C).

10.12.4 An air heater installed inside a building shall be provided with a chimney connector to conduct the flue gases to the outside.

10.12.5 Flexible ducts shall be made of material resistant to heat and flame and that can withstand prolonged exposure to temperatures as high as 250°F (121°C).

10.13 Specific Requirements for Recessed Wall Furnaces.

10.13.1 Listed recessed wall furnaces shall be permitted to be installed in walls of combustible construction.

10.13.2 The authority having jurisdiction shall be consulted for the proper installation methods to be followed.

10.13.3 Recessed wall furnaces shall be installed in accordance with the manufacturers' instructions.

10.13.4 Recessed wall furnaces shall be located so as not to cause a hazard to walls, floors, curtains, furniture, doors, and so forth.

10.13.5 The face of a warm-air register shall be at least 3 ft (0.9 m) from any wall or combustible surface that is directly opposite the register.

10.13.6 Panels, grilles, and access doors that must be removed for normal servicing operations shall not be attached to the building construction.

10.13.7 Adequate combustion and circulating air shall be provided.

10.14 Specific Requirements for Floor-Mounted Restaurant-Type Cooking Appliances.

10.14.1 Floor-mounted restaurant-type cooking appliances shall be installed with clearances to combustible material of not less than 18 in. (450 mm) at the sides and rear of the appliance and from the chimney connector thereof and not less than 4 ft (1.2 m) above the cooking top and at the front of the appliance.

10.14.2 Floor-mounted restaurant-type cooking appliances that are listed for installation with lesser clearances than specified in 10.14.1 shall be permitted to be installed in accordance with the conditions of their listing.

10.14.3 Floor-mounted restaurant-type cooking appliances shall be permitted to be installed in rooms, but not in confined spaces such as alcoves, with lesser clearance to woodwork or other combustible material, provided the combustible material is protected as specified by Table 10.6.2, Protection Types (c), (e), and (g).

10.14.4 Where a wall or cabinet of combustible material is located adjacent to the cooking top section of the appliance and is not shielded from the cooking top section by a high shelf, warming closet, or other such part of the appliance, the protection specified in 10.14.3 shall extend for a distance of at least 2 ft (0.6 m) above the surface of the cooking top.

10.14.4.1 Such wall or cabinet shall be protected even though the appliance is listed for "close-to-the-wall" installation.

10.14.5 Floor-mounted appliances shall be placed in either of the following ways:

(1) On floors of fire-resistive construction with noncombustible flooring or surface finish and with no combustible material against the underside thereof
(2) On fire-resistive slabs or arches having no combustible material against the underside thereof, with such construction in all cases extending not less than 12 in. (300 mm) beyond the appliance on all sides

10.14.5.1 Floor-mounted appliances that are specifically listed for installation on a floor constructed of combustible material shall be permitted to be placed in accordance with the conditions of their listing.

10.14.5.2 Floor-mounted appliances shall be permitted to be placed on combustible floors although not listed for such installation, provided the floor under the appliance is protected in accordance with the requirements of accepted building code practice.

10.15 Specific Requirements for Suspended-Type Unit Heaters.

10.15.1 Suspended-type unit heaters shall be installed with clearances to combustible material not less than those specified by Table 10.6.1.

10.15.1.1 Suspended-type unit heaters that are listed for installation with lesser clearances shall be permitted to be installed in accordance with their listing.

10.15.1.2 Suspended-type unit heaters shall be permitted to be installed with lesser clearances to combustible material, provided the combustible material is protected as specified by Table 10.6.2 and Figure 10.6.2(a), Figure 10.6.2(b), and Figure 10.6.2(c).

10.15.2 Suspended-type heaters shall be safely and adequately supported.

10.15.3 Hangers or brackets supporting heaters shall be metal.

10.15.4 The location of any suspended unit heater or its ductwork shall be such that a negative pressure will not be created in the room where the unit heater is located.

10.15.5 A suspended unit heater shall not be attached to a warm-air duct system unless listed for such installation.

10.16 Specific Requirements for Direct-Vent Appliances. (Reserved)

10.17 Specific Requirements for Appliances on Roofs.

10.17.1 Appliances installed on roofs shall be designed or enclosed to withstand expected climate conditions.

10.17.2 If the appliance is enclosed, the enclosure shall permit easy entry and movement, shall be of reasonable height, and shall have at least a 30 in. (750 mm) clearance between the entire service access panel of the equipment and the wall of the enclosure.

10.17.3 The roof where the appliance is to be installed shall be capable of supporting the additional load or shall be reinforced to support the additional load.

10.17.4 All access locks, screws, and bolts shall be of corrosion-resistant material.

10.17.5 Appliances shall be installed in accordance with their listings and with manufacturers' instructions.

10.17.6 Appliances shall be installed on a well-drained surface of the roof.

10.17.7 At least 6 ft (1.8 m) of clearance shall be maintained between any part of the appliance and the edge of the roof or similar hazard.

Exception: Rigidly fixed rails or guards at least 42 in. (1 m) high shall be permitted to be used as an alternate to the 6 ft (1.8 m) clearance. Parapets or other parts of the building structure that are at least 42 in. (1 m) high shall be permitted to be used in lieu of rails or guards.

10.17.8 Appliances requiring an external source of electrical power shall be provided with a readily accessible electrical disconnect that will completely de-energize the equipment.

10.17.8.1 This disconnect shall be installed within sight of the equipment.

10.17.8.2 A 120-volt ac grounding-type receptacle outlet shall be provided adjacent to the equipment.

10.17.8.3 This receptacle outlet shall be connected to the supply side of the electrical disconnect.

10.17.9 Where water stands on the roof at the equipment or in the passageways leading to the equipment or where the roof is of a water-sealed design, a suitable platform or walkway or both shall be provided above the water line and adjacent to the equipment and the control panels so that equipment can be safely serviced.

10.17.10 Appliances located on roofs or other elevated platforms shall be accessible.

10.18 Installation of Outdoor Appliances.

10.18.1 Appliances listed for outdoor installation shall be permitted to be installed without additional environmental protection in accordance with the terms of their listing and shall be accessible for servicing.

10.18.2 Appliances that are not listed for outdoor installation shall be permitted to be installed outdoors if approved for such installation.

10.18.2.1 In determining suitability for outdoor installation, the following factors shall be considered:

(1) Protection from physical damage
(2) Location of combustion air and other openings into the appliance
(3) Surface temperatures
(4) Weatherproofing
(5) Adequate and safe venting
(6) Clearances to adjacent combustibles

Chapter 11 Installation and Operation of Oil-Burning Stoves, Kerosene-Burning Room Heaters, and Kerosene-Burning Portable Heaters

11.1 Scope. This chapter shall apply to the installation and operation of oil-burning stoves, kerosene-burning room heaters, and kerosene-burning portable heaters.

11.2* Basic Requirements.

11.2.1 Appliances shall be kept clean and in good repair. The following requirements also shall apply:

(1) When necessary, repairs or replacement of parts shall be done by the manufacturer or the manufacturer's representative.
(2) Where repair or replacement of parts must be done by the user, it shall be strictly confined to procedures that have been fully covered by the manufacturer's printed instructions.

11.2.2 Instructions furnished by the manufacturer shall be preserved.

11.2.3 Special care shall be employed in the installation of oil-burning stoves, kerosene-burning room heaters, and kerosene-burning portable heaters in order to avoid direct contact with combustible material, including draperies and curtains, and to avoid accidental overturning.

11.2.4 Appliances shall be carefully leveled in accordance with manufacturers' installation instructions.

11.2.5 Where manufacturers' instructions specify that oil-burning stoves and kerosene-burning room heaters are to be fastened to the floor, these instructions shall be carefully followed.

11.2.6 In all cases, oil-burning stoves and kerosene-burning heaters that are supplied with fuel from separate supply tanks shall be securely attached to the floor or otherwise secured in position to avoid strains on piping.

11.2.7 The filling of removable tanks for oil-burning stoves and kerosene-burning portable heaters shall be done outside of buildings or at a special location where precautions can be taken to minimize fuel spills.

11.2.8 Flue Connections. Appliances that are intended for connection to a flue shall be connected to a suitable chimney or integral appliance venting system to ensure having sufficient draft at all times. *(See Section 6.6.)*

11.2.9 Fuel Supply Tanks.

11.2.9.1 Oil-burning stoves and kerosene-burning room heaters designed for gravity feed shall not be connected to separate supply tanks or lift pumps.

11.2.9.2 Oil-burning stoves and kerosene-burning room heaters specifically designed and listed for use with separate supply tanks shall be permitted to be connected for gravity feed from a supply tank or an automatic pump.

11.2.9.3 Tanks supplying oil-burning stoves and kerosene-burning room heaters by gravity feed shall be installed in such a way that the pressure at the fuel supply tank will not be greater than the pressure at a point 8 ft (2.4 m) above the appliance's fuel inlet connection and shall be installed in accordance with the applicable requirements in Chapter 7.

11.2.10 Automatic lift pumps shall be securely mounted and shall be equipped with an overflow line that returns to the supply tank. The oil piping shall comply with the applicable requirements in Chapter 8.

11.2.11 Clearances and Mounting.

11.2.11.1 Oil-burning stoves, kerosene-burning room heaters, and kerosene-burning portable heaters shall be installed to provide clearances to combustible material not less than those specified by Table 11.2.11.1.

Table 11.2.11.1 Minimum Clearances for Heating and Cooking Appliances

| Appliances | Minimum Clearance (in.) | | |
	Sides	Rear	Chimney Connector
Oil-burning stoves	24	9	18
Kerosene-burning room heaters	18	18	18
Kerosene-burning portable heaters of the radiant or convection type	36	36	Not applicable

For SI units, 1 in. = 25 mm, 1 ft = 0.3 m.

11.2.11.2 Oil-burning stoves, kerosene-burning room heaters, and kerosene-burning portable heaters that are listed for installation with lesser clearances than specified in Table 11.2.11.1 shall be permitted to be installed in accordance with their listing.

11.2.11.3 Oil-burning stoves and kerosene-burning room heaters shall be permitted to be installed with lesser clearances to combustible material, provided the combustible material is protected as described in Table 10.6.2 and Figure 10.6.2(a), Figure 10.6.2(b), and Figure 10.6.2(c).

11.2.11.4 In no case shall the horizontal distance be less than 6 in. (150 mm) from an oil-burning stove to that portion of adjacent unprotected combustible walls or cabinets extending above the cooking top of the range portion of the oil-burning stove.

11.2.11.5 Oil-burning stoves shall have a clearance vertically above the top of not less than 30 in. (750 mm) to combustible material or cabinets.

11.2.11.5.1 Where the underside of combustible material or cabinets is protected by fire-resistive board at least 1.4 in. (6 mm) thick covered with sheet metal not lighter than 28 gauge, the distance shall be at least 24 in. (600 mm).

11.2.11.5.2 The protection shall extend 9 in. (225 mm) beyond the sides of the oil-burning stove.

11.2.11.6 Listed kerosene-burning portable heaters shall be permitted to be placed on combustible floors.

11.2.11.7 Oil-burning stoves and kerosene-burning room heaters shall be placed on noncombustible floors or on floors protected in accordance with accepted building code practice, unless listed for installation on combustible flooring.

11.3 Additional Requirements for Kerosene-Burning Portable Heaters.

11.3.1* Kerosene-burning portable heaters shall be listed.

11.3.2 Extreme caution shall be exercised in the placement and use of these devices since surface temperatures can be sufficient to cause contact burns and the device can constitute a source of ignition in the presence of flammable vapors.

Chapter 12   Used Oil–Burning Appliances

12.1 Scope. This chapter shall apply to appliances that burn used oil as a fuel.

12.2 Basic Requirements. Used oil–burning appliances shall meet the requirements of this chapter and all applicable requirements of Chapters 4 through 8 and Chapters 10 and 11 of this standard.

12.3 Use of Used Oil–Burning Appliances. Used oil–burning appliances shall be used only in commercial or industrial occupancies. They shall not be used in a residential occupancy.

12.4 Listing Requirements.

12.4.1 Used oil–burning appliances shall be listed in accordance with ANSI/UL 296A, *Standard for Waste Oil-Burning Air Heating Appliances*.

12.4.2* The listing of the used oil–burning appliance shall apply to the used oil burner and the end-use appliance together as a single listed product.

12.4.3 A burner shall not be used for firing used oil unless the burner is covered together with the end-use appliance as a single listed product.

12.5 Installation Instructions.

12.5.1 The user shall preserve the installation and operation instructions provided with the used oil–burning appliance at the site where the appliance is operated.

12.5.2 The installation and operation instructions provided with the used oil–burning appliance shall include a statement to the effect that the used oil–burning appliance is to be installed by a qualified person.

12.6 Installation Clearances.

12.6.1 The installation of a used oil–burning appliance shall meet the appropriate clearances to combustible construction that are specified in Chapter 10.

12.6.2 Used oil–burning appliances shall be separated from flammable or combustible liquids in accordance with applicable requirements of NFPA 30A, *Code for Motor Fuel Dispensing Facilities and Repair Garages*.

12.7 Burners for Used Oil–Burning Appliances.

12.7.1 Fuel Supply.

12.7.1.1 A readily accessible manual shutoff valve shall be provided downstream of the used oil supply tank.

12.7.1.2 A properly sized and rated oil filter or strainer shall be installed in the used oil supply line to the used oil burner.

12.7.1.2.1 The oil filter or strainer shall be downstream of the shutoff valve specified in 12.7.1.1 and upstream of the fuel pump of the used oil burner.

12.7.1.2.2 The oil filter or strainer shall be removable for inspection and cleaning.

12.7.2 Atomization Air Supply for Air-Atomized Burners.

12.7.2.1 The atomization air supply for an air-atomized burner shall be taken from a source that is reasonably constant in pressure and volume.

12.7.2.1.1 An atomization air supply that is covered as part of a listed used oil burner and used oil–fired appliance combination — for example, an air compressor — shall be deemed as meeting this requirement.

12.7.2.2 If shop air is used as the atomization air supply, the installation shall comply with the following:

(1) A manual shutoff valve shall be provided upstream of the atomization air supply connection to the used oil burner that will allow the used oil burner and used oil–burning appliance to be serviced without having to interrupt the shop air supply.
(2) When the shop air supply pressure is greater than the rated atomization air pressure for the used oil burner, the manual shutoff valve specified in 12.7.2.2(1) shall be followed by a suitable air pressure regulator that will allow atomization air to be supplied at the pressure(s) marked on the used oil burner or used oil–burning appliance.
(3) A suitably rated filter and condensate trap system shall be provided upstream of the atomization air supply connection to the used oil burner, but downstream of the manual valve specified in 12.7.2.2(1) or downstream of the atomization air pressure regulator, if provided.
(4) The air intake to the shop air source shall be reasonably free of carbon monoxide contamination.

12.8 Venting of Combustion (Flue) Gases. A used oil–burning appliance shall be vented in accordance with the manufacturers' instructions that are provided with the appliance. The requirements of 12.8.1 and 12.8.2 shall also apply and shall supersede the manufacturers' instructions.

12.8.1 The venting system for a used oil–burning appliance shall meet all applicable requirements of Chapter 6 of this standard.

12.8.2 A vent connector or vent manifold serving two or more used oil–burning appliances shall have an effective cross-sectional area that is not less than the combined cross-sectional area of the individual flue collars or individual connectors of all appliances served, unless the vent connector or vent manifold complies with 12.8.3.

12.8.3 A vent connector or vent manifold serving two or more used oil–burning appliances shall be permitted to have an effective cross-sectional area that is less than that specified in 12.8.2 if all of the following conditions are met:

(1) The configuration of the manifolded vent connectors are covered as part of the appliance listing.
(2) The transition piece that joins all of the vent connectors or vent manifolds is provided with the appliance.
(3) The manifolded vent is installed in accordance with the manufacturers' installation and operation instructions provided with the appliance and in accordance with the terms of its listing.

12.9 Used Oil Supply Tanks.

12.9.1 Supply tanks for aboveground indoor supply of used oil to a used oil–burning appliance shall be listed in accordance with ANSI/UL 80, *Standard for Steel Tanks for Oil-Burner Fuels and Other Combustible Liquids*, or ANSI/UL 142, *Standard for Steel Aboveground Tanks for Flammable and Combustible Liquids*.

12.9.2 Secondary containment-type tanks meeting the requirements of 7.2.7.1 and listed for use with used oil shall be permitted to be used for aboveground, indoor supply.

12.9.3 Supply tanks for aboveground indoor supply of used oil to a used oil–burning appliance shall be listed in accordance with ANSI/UL 80, *Standard for Steel Tanks for Oil-Burner Fuels and Other Combustible Liquids*, or ANSI/UL 142, *Standard for Steel Aboveground Tanks for Flammable and Combustible Liquids*.

12.9.4 Supply tanks for underground supply of used oil to a used oil–burning appliance shall be listed in accordance with UL 58, *Standard for Steel Underground Tanks for Flammable and Combustible Liquids*, or UL 1316, *Standard for Glass-Fiber Reinforced Plastic Underground Storage Tanks for Petroleum Products, Alcohols and Alcohol-Gasoline Mixtures*.

12.9.5 Supply tanks for supply of used oil to a used oil–burning appliance shall meet all other applicable requirements of Chapter 7 of this standard.

12.10 Piping, Pumps, and Valves.

12.10.1 Pumps, valves, and other ancillary equipment for transferring or storing used oil shall be listed and shall be suitable for use with the types of used oil intended to be fired.

12.10.2 Piping for transferring used oil to the used oil–burning appliance shall meet all applicable requirements of Chapter 8 of this standard.

12.11 Operating Requirements.

12.11.1 Only the types of used oil designated on the marking of the used oil burner or used oil–burning appliance shall be used.

12.11.2 Other types of used oil that are not designated on the marking of the burner or the appliance shall not be used and shall not be mixed with the types of used oil that are intended for use.

12.12 Vent Connector and Chimney Inspection. Prior to and after installation of the used oil–burning appliance, consideration shall be given to inspecting the vent connector and the chimney serving the appliance. *(See Annex E, Relining Masonry Chimneys.)*

12.13 U.S. Environmental Protection Agency Regulations. Regulations of the U.S. Environmental Protection Agency, as specified in 40 CFR 279.23, "On-Site Burning in Space Heaters," for the locality of the area where the used oil–burning appliance is operated shall be met. The following requirements shall also apply:

(1) The used oil–burning appliance shall burn only used oils that the owner or operator of the appliance generates on the site where the appliance is operated, or used oils that are received from household do-it-yourself used oil generators.
(2)*The used oil–burning appliance shall not have a maximum input rate exceeding 500,000 Btu/hr (approximately 3.6 gal/hr) (527,500 kW).
(3) The combustion gases from the used oil–burning appliance shall be vented to the outdoors.

Chapter 13 Oil-and-Gas–Burning Appliances

13.1 Scope.

13.1.1 This chapter shall apply to appliances that are capable of burning either fuel oils or fuel gases as a main fuel source in an alternate manner, such as burners, furnaces, boilers, and so forth.

13.1.2 Oil-and-gas–burning appliances shall be used only in commercial 400,000 Btu/hr (117 kW) or industrial applications and installations.

13.2 Listing Requirements. An oil-and-gas–burning appliance and the burner of an oil-and-gas–burning appliance, either as part of the appliance or separately, shall be listed.

13.3 Installation, Operation, and Servicing Instructions.

13.3.1 Installation, operation, and servicing instructions for an oil-and-gas–burning appliance shall be preserved by the user.

13.3.2 The installation, operation, and servicing instructions furnished with an oil-and-gas–burning appliance shall include a statement to the effect that the oil-and-gas–burning appliance shall be installed and serviced by a qualified person.

13.3.3 A description of the method for changing the fuel supply to the appliance from oil to gas and vice versa shall be included in the installation, operation, and servicing instructions furnished with the appliance.

13.4 Clearances from Oil–Gas-Fired Appliance to Combustible Material.

13.4.1 Clearances from combustible materials shall be as specified in Chapter 10 of this standard and in NFPA 54, *National Fuel Gas Code*, for the specific type of appliance.

13.4.2 Where there is a difference between the clearances required by Chapter 10 of this standard and those required by NFPA 54, *National Fuel Gas Code*, for a particular appliance, the greater clearance shall apply.

13.5 Construction.

13.5.1 The burner of an oil-and-gas–burning appliance shall be arranged so that the main burner fuel not being fired will be shut off automatically when the main burner is not in its intended firing position for that fuel.

13.5.2 The burner of an oil-and-gas–burning appliance shall be arranged so that the fuel being fired is shut off before the other fuel is delivered to the ignition zone.

13.5.3 Prior to ignition of the main burner fuel from either a cold start or a fuel changeover, the burner ignition system shall provide a predetermined ignition cycle for the fuel to be fired.

13.5.3.1 The predetermined ignition cycle shall include the applicable pre-purge period, trial for ignition period, pilot flame establishing period, and main burner flame establishing period as specified in ANSI/UL 296, *Standard for Oil Burners*, and UL 795, *Standard for Commercial Industrial Gas-Heating Equipment.*

13.5.4 The burner of an oil-and-gas appliance shall be arranged so that the maximum rated Btu/hr capacity of the burner does not exceed the maximum rated operating Btu/hr input of the appliance, regardless of the fuel being fired.

13.5.5 Changeover of the main burner fuel source shall be accomplished without manual adjustment of the appliance unless such adjustment is interlocked to provide safety shutdown of the appliance should misadjustment occur.

13.5.6 Fuel-handling components of an oil-and-gas burner and an oil-and-gas–burning appliance shall meet all applicable requirements of the standards under which they are manufactured.

13.5.7 Fuel-handling components of an oil-and-gas burner and an oil-and-gas–burning appliance shall be suitable for the intended application with respect to the type of fuel being handled and the exposed temperatures and pressures that the fuel-handling component will be subjected to in service.

13.6 Flue Connections.

13.6.1 The venting system of an oil-and-gas–burning appliance shall meet all applicable requirements of this standard and of NFPA 54, *National Fuel Gas Code.*

13.6.2 Where requirements for venting differ between this standard and NFPA 54, *National Fuel Gas Code*, the more stringent requirements shall apply.

13.7 Piping, Pumps, and Valves. Piping for fuel oil shall meet all applicable requirements of Chapter 8 of this standard. Piping for fuel gas shall meet all applicable requirements of NFPA 54, *National Fuel Gas Code.*

13.8 Performance. An oil-and-gas burner and its appliance shall be capable of operation when firing each type of fuel for which the equipment is rated as marked on its respective nameplate.

13.9 Testing. Upon installation, an oil-and-gas burner and its appliance shall be tested for proper operation and combustion characteristics with each fuel, in accordance with its installation, operating, and servicing instructions and as required by the authority having jurisdiction.

Annex A   Explanatory Material

Annex A is not a part of the requirements of this NFPA document but is included for informational purposes only. This annex contains explanatory material, numbered to correspond with the applicable text paragraphs.

A.1.1.5 Examples of portable devices not covered by this standard are blowtorches, melting pots, and weed burners.

A.3.2.1 Approved. The National Fire Protection Association does not approve, inspect, or certify any installations, procedures, equipment, or materials; nor does it approve or evaluate testing laboratories. In determining the acceptability of installations, procedures, equipment, or materials, the authority having jurisdiction may base acceptance on compliance with NFPA or other appropriate standards. In the absence of such standards, said authority may require evidence of proper installation, procedure, or use. The authority having jurisdiction may also refer to the listings or labeling practices of an organization that is concerned with product evaluations and is thus in a position to determine compliance with appropriate standards for the current production of listed items.

A.3.2.2 Authority Having Jurisdiction (AHJ). The phrase "authority having jurisdiction," or its acronym AHJ, is used in NFPA documents in a broad manner, since jurisdictions and approval agencies vary, as do their responsibilities. Where public safety is primary, the authority having jurisdiction may be a federal, state, local, or other regional department or individual such as a fire chief; fire marshal; chief of a fire prevention bureau, labor department, or health department; building official; electrical inspector; or others having statutory authority. For insurance purposes, an insurance inspection department, rating bureau, or other insurance company representative may be the authority having jurisdiction. In many circumstances, the property owner or his or her designated agent assumes the role of the authority having jurisdiction; at government installations, the commanding officer or departmental official may be the authority having jurisdiction.

A.3.2.4 Listed. The means for identifying listed equipment may vary for each organization concerned with product evaluation;

some organizations do not recognize equipment as listed unless it is also labeled. The authority having jurisdiction should utilize the system employed by the listing organization to identify a listed product.

A.3.3.7 Central Heating Appliance. A floor-mounted unit heater connected to a duct system is also classified as a central heating appliance.

A.3.3.24.1 Mechanical Draft. When the mechanical means is applied to *push* the flue gases through the chimney or vent system, the draft is *forced.* When the mechanical means is applied to *pull* the flue gases through the chimney or vent system, the draft is *induced.*

A.3.3.28.7 Floor Furnace. A fuel-burning floor furnace is designed to take air for combustion from outside the space being heated and is provided with means for observing the flame and lighting the appliance from such space.

A.3.3.30 Heating and Cooking Appliance. These appliances include kerosene stoves, oil stoves, portable kerosene heaters, and conversion range oil burners.

A.3.3.37 Liquid Fuel. Fuel oil used for the typical liquid fuel–burning appliance has a flash point ranging from 100°F to 145°F (38°C to 63°C) and would be designated a Class II or Class IIIA combustible liquid, in accordance with NFPA 30, *Flammable and Combustible Liquids Code.*

A.3.3.41 Oil Burner. A burner of this type can be furnished with or without a primary safety control, and it can be a pressure-atomizing gun type, a horizontal or vertical rotary type, or a mechanical or natural draft vaporizing type.

A.3.3.42 Oil-Burning Appliance (Oil-Burning Unit). This definition does not include kerosene stoves or oil stoves.

A.3.3.44 Oil-Burning Stove. An oil-burning stove can be equipped with an integral oil tank or can be designed for connection to a separate oil supply tank.

A.3.3.53.1 Circulating Room Heater. Room heaters that have openings in an outer jacket to allow some direct radiation from the heat exchanger are classified as a radiant type.

A.3.3.57.1 Oil Burner Auxiliary Tank. An auxiliary tank can be included as an integral part of an automatic pump or a transfer pump, or it can be a separate tank.

A.3.3.60 Unconfined Space. Rooms connecting directly with the space in which the appliances are located by means of openings that have no doors or closures, unless fully louvered, are considered part of the unconfined space.

A.3.3.61 Unit Heater. A unit heater can be either direct-fired or indirect-fired using steam, hot water, or electricity.

A.3.3.65 Venting System (Flue Gases). A venting system for exhausting flue gases usually is composed of a gas vent, Type L vent, or a chimney and vent or chimney connector(s), if used, assembled to form the open passageway.

A.3.3.66 Wall Furnace. Wall furnaces should not be provided with duct extensions beyond the vertical and horizontal limits of the casing proper, except that boots not exceeding 10 in. (250 mm) beyond the horizontal of the casing for extension through walls of nominal thickness are permitted. Where provided, such boots should be supplied by the manufacturer as an integral part of the appliance. This definition excludes floor furnaces, unit heaters, and central furnaces.

A.4.5.1 See Chapter 11 for additional requirements for oil-burning stoves, kerosene-burning room heaters, and kerosene-burning portable heaters. See Chapter 12 for additional requirements for used oil–burning appliances. See Chapter 13 for additional requirements for combination oil-and-gas–burning appliances.

A.4.5.3 Where heavy oils are used, provisions should be made to maintain the oil within the recommended temperature range indicated in Table A.4.5.3, so that proper atomization is maintained.

Table A.4.5.3 Recommended Temperature Range for Proper Atomization of Heavy Oils

Fuel No.	Viscosity in SSU at 100°F	Low Temperature Limit (°F)	High Temperature Limit (°F)
4	45	35*	50
	50	35*	65
	60	45*	85
	75	62	105
	100	80	125
5	150	100	145
	200	112	160
	300	130	180
	400	140	190
	500	150	200
6	1,000	170	225
	2,000	190	245
	3,000	205	260
	4,000	212	270
	5,000	218	275
	10,000	240	290

*At these temperatures, proper operation of the appliance might not be attained because of unsatisfactory atomization of the fuel. For this reason, the fuel oil should be kept at the high end of the recommended temperature range.

A.4.5.3(4) ANSI/UL 296A, *Standard for Waste Oil-Burning Air Heating Appliances,* specifies that a burner provided with preheating means for the fuel oil can be provided with an oil temperature interlock device to prevent delivery of the fuel oil to the firing portion of the burner until the fuel oil has reached a predetermined minimum temperature. On a burner that is not equipped with oil-preheating equipment, an oil temperature interlock device should not be provided on the burner and should be bypassed during any firing tests of the burner.

A.4.6.1 Typical locations are burner areas, fuel-handling areas, fuel storage areas, pits, sumps, and low spots where fuel leakage or vapors can accumulate. Chapter 5 of *NFPA 70, National Electrical Code,* provides information for classifying such areas and defines requirements for electrical installations in areas so classified.

Crankcase oil and used oil properties can vary considerably, and light volatile materials can be released during storage or handling or upon heating. Because of this characteristic, appropriate and adequate provisions should be made to safely handle, store, and burn crankcase oil and used oil. It is desirable that flexibility be built into the facility to accommodate the expected range of properties. Failure to observe the necessary design, installation, and operating and maintenance procedures can result in fire, explosion, or personal injury.

Extensive treatment of this subject is beyond the scope of this standard. The authority having jurisdiction should be responsible for classifying areas where fuel is stored, handled, or burned, and for revising the classification if conditions are changed. Installation should conform to *NFPA 70, National Electrical Code.* Additional guidance can be obtained from NFPA 30, *Flammable and Combustible Liquids Code*, and NFPA 30A, *Code for Motor Fuel Dispensing Facilities and Repair Garages.*

A.4.6.4 Required ventilation of areas where crankcase oil burning and used oil–burning appliances operate depends on the type of area where the equipment is located. For example, NFPA 30A, *Code for Motor Fuel Dispensing Facilities and Repair Garages*, requires 1 cfm/ft^2 (0.3 m^3/min/m^2) of floor area be provided based on the dispensing area for fuel-dispensing areas inside buildings. Additional guidance can be found in Chapter 5 of NFPA 30, *Flammable and Combustible Liquids Code.*

A.5.3.1 In buildings of conventional construction, normal infiltration is generally sufficient to provide the necessary air for proper combustion and ventilation.

A.5.8 Depressurization of houses by operating combustion equipment as well as by operation of exhaust fans, kitchen exhausts, whole-house fans, clothes dryers, fireplaces, and so forth, can adversely impact the operation and safety of oil-burning equipment. Houses vary widely with respect to depressurization, and newer, more tightly constructed houses are particularly susceptible. While Section 5.8 requires various methods for supplying combustion and draft dilution air, mechanical ventilation systems are now being produced that supply makeup air from outside. Where a mechanical combustion air system is used to provide combustion and dilution, provisions should be made to prevent operation of the oil burner(s) where the combustion and dilution air system is not performing, so as to satisfy the safe operating requirements of the equipment.

A.6.3.1 A natural-draft burner, as defined herein, should be connected to an individual chimney or chimney flue used for no other appliance.

A.6.3.4 Some corrective steps that can be taken to reduce chimney downdraft include, but are not limited to, the following:

(1) Extension of the existing chimney
(2) Installation or replacement of the chimney cap
(3) Installation of a draft fan
(4) Determination that adequate combustion air is being provided
(5) Inspection of the chimney to determine if the passageway is blocked
(6) Relining the flue with a listed chimney lining system *(See Annex E.)*
(7) Installation of an insulated vent connector
(8) A check for depressurization of the building due to other exhaust fans, ventilation fans, and so forth and correction of any deficiencies

A.6.6.6 See Annex C for diagrams showing typical installations.

A.6.6.7 If the chimney or flue gas venting system shows signs of deterioration or is unlined and the oil-burning appliance is maintaining the proper draft as specified by the manufacturer, the appliance can be installed while awaiting the inspection and proper maintenance to be accomplished, as required by Chapter 13 of NFPA 211, *Standard for Chimneys, Fireplaces, Vents, and Solid Fuel–Burning Appliances.*

A.6.6.8 This might require repair, relining, or resizing of the chimney flue. See Annex E for additional information.

A.6.6.9 See Annex E for recommendations and venting tables for relined masonry chimneys.

A.6.7.3 Figure A.6.7.3 illustrates the application of the requirements of 6.7.3.

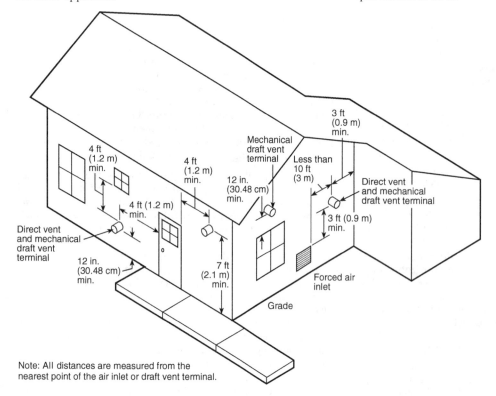

Note: All distances are measured from the nearest point of the air inlet or draft vent terminal.

FIGURE A.6.7.3   Exit Terminals of Mechanical Draft and Direct Venting Systems.

A.7.2.7.6 See UL 1316, *Standard for Glass-Fiber-Reinforced Plastic Underground Storage Tanks for Petroleum Products, Alcohols, and Alcohol-Gasoline Mixtures*; UL 1746, *Standard for External Corrosion Protection Systems for Steel Underground Storage Tanks*; and STI ACT-100, *Specification for External Corrosion Protection of FRP Composite Steel Underground Tanks, F894*.

A.7.2.7.7 The type of vault being referred to in this paragraph is *not* the same as that referred to in 7.5.13.3 or 7.5.13.4.

A.7.3.1 Appendix E of API Standard 650, *Welded Steel Tanks for Oil Storage*, provides information on tank foundations.

A.7.4.5 For additional information, see PEI RP-100, *Recommended Practices for Installation of Underground Liquid Storage Systems*.

A.7.4.7 See Annex C of NFPA 30, *Flammable and Combustible Liquids Code*.

A.7.8.4 Primer paints do not qualify as suitable corrosion protection. The asphaltum coating or rust-inhibiting material typically used on outside tanks does meet the intent of this requirement for external corrosion protection.

A.7.9.2 Tank heaters connected so that condensate or water is not returned to the boiler are preferred.

A.10.5.1 There should be an approved device installed above the unit to stop the flow of electrical current through the safety control circuit under conditions of excessive temperature in the room where the oil-burning unit is located. It should be of the type that requires replacement of the trip component to reactivate the unit when the device has tripped due to excessive temperature. Units that are installed outdoors and unenclosed are exempt from this recommendation.

A.10.5.3 See ASME CSD-1, *Controls and Safety Devices for Automatically Fired Boilers*, and ANSI/UL 296, *Standard for Oil Burners*, for further information. Primary safety controls for burners can consist of a combustion-type electrical control or an antiflooding device. The proper control to be furnished with each burner is indicated in the listing by the testing agency.

A.10.5.4 The quantity and the specific operating characteristics for limit controls will vary, depending on the type of appliance and the requirements of the authority having jurisdiction. For information purposes only, the limit control requirements of applicable standards and from ASME CSD-1, *Controls and Safety Devices for Automatically Fired Boilers*, are presented in Table A.10.5.4. This information is provided only for limit controls that safeguard pressure and low water level in a steam boiler, that safeguard low water level and over-temperature in a water boiler, and that safeguard over-temperature in furnaces and heaters. Additional limit controls and operating controls (e.g., a fan control on a furnace) are usually required to safeguard other operational characteristics of the appliance. The user of this standard is advised to refer to the applicable standards and to the authority having jurisdiction for specific requirements and details.

Table A.10.5.4 Limit Control Requirements from Various Standards

| Appliance Type | Characteristic of Appliance to Protect | Limit Control Required | | Standard References(s) |
		Limit Control Description	General Operational Characteristics of Limit Control	
Boiler, high pressure steam	Low water level	Two low water level limit controls or two combination water feed controls and low water level limit controls. Both low water level limit controls should be electrically wired so that operation of either control causes fuel cutoff to the burner. One of the low water level limit controls should be set to function at a lower water level than the other low water level limit control. The upper low water level limit control can be of the automatic reset or manual reset type. The lower low water level limit control should be of the manual reset type and should require local manual intervention to reset. A miniature boiler* should be provided with one manual reset type low water level limit control or one combination water feed control and manual reset type low water level limit control. The low water level limit control should require local manual intervention to reset.	All low water level limit controls should cause fuel cutoff to the burner before the water level in the boiler falls below the lowest visible part of the gauge glass. Fuel cutoff to the burner and safety shut down can occur simultaneously with the low water level limit control functioning to shut down the burner, or it can incorporate a time delay to prevent short cycling. The time delay should not exceed the boiler manufacturers' recommended time or 90 seconds, whichever is less.	UL 726, *Standard for Oil-Fired Boiler Assemblies* ASME CSD-1, *Controls and Safety Devices for Automatically Fired Boilers*

Table A.10.5.4 *Continued*

| Appliance Type | Characteristic of Appliance to Protect | Limit Control Required | | Standard References(s) |
		Limit Control Description	General Operational Characteristics of Limit Control	
Boiler, high pressure steam, *continued*	High steam pressure	One manual reset–type limit control, which requires local manual intervention to reset.	When adjusted to its maximum setting allowed by a fixed stop, the limit control should limit the steam pressure to not more than the maximum allowable working pressure of the boiler.	UL 726, *Standard for Oil-Fired Boiler Assemblies* ASME CSD-1, *Controls and Safety Devices for Automatically Fired Boilers*
		For a boiler installed in a residence as defined by the authority having jurisdiction, the high steam pressure limit control is not required to have local manual intervention to reset and can instead have automatic reset.		ASME CSD-1, *Controls and Safety Devices for Automatically Fired Boilers*
Boiler, low pressure steam	Low water level	Two low water level limit controls or two combination water feed controls and low water level limit controls. Both low water level limit controls should be electrically wired so that operation of either control causes fuel cutoff to the burner. One of the low water level limit controls should be set to function at a lower water level than the other low water level limit control. The upper low water level limit control can be of the automatic reset or manual reset type. The lower low water level limit control should be of the manual reset type and should require local manual intervention to reset. A miniature boiler* should be provided with one manual reset–type low water level limit control or one combination water feed control and manual reset type low water level limit control. The low water level limit control should require local manual intervention to reset. For a gravity return boiler installed in a residence as defined by the authority having jurisdiction, only one low water limit control or one combination water feed control and low water level limit control is required. This low water level limit control should require local manual intervention to reset.	All low water level limit controls should cause fuel cutoff to the burner before the water level in the boiler falls below the lowest visible part of the gauge glass. Fuel cutoff to the burner and safety shut down can occur simultaneously with the low water level limit control functioning to shut down the burner, or it can incorporate a time delay to prevent short cycling. The time delay should not exceed the boiler manufacturers' recommended time or 90 seconds, whichever is less.	UL 726, *Standard for Oil-Fired Boiler Assemblies* ASME CSD-1, *Controls and Safety Devices for Automatically Fired Boilers* ASME CSD-1, *Controls and Safety Devices for Automatically Fired Boilers*

Table A.10.5.4 *Continued*

Appliance Type	Characteristic of Appliance to Protect	Limit Control Required		Standard References(s)
		Limit Control Description	**General Operational Characteristics of Limit Control**	
	High steam pressure	One manual reset–type limit control, which requires local manual intervention to reset.	When adjusted to its maximum setting allowed by a fixed stop, the limit control should limit the steam pressure to not more than a gauge pressure of 15 psi (103 kPa).	UL 726, *Standard for Oil-Fired Boiler Assemblies* ASME CSD-1, *Controls and Safety Devices for Automatically Fired Boilers*
		For a boiler installed in a residence as defined by the authority having jurisdiction, the high steam pressure limit control is not required to have local manual intervention to reset and can instead have automatic reset.		ASME CSD-1, *Controls and Safety Devices for Automatically Fired Boilers*
Boiler, water	Low water level	One manual reset–type low water level limit control or one combination water feed control and manual reset type low water level limit–control. The low water level limit control should require local manual intervention to reset. A tube or coil-type water boiler that requires forced water circulation can instead employ an automatic reset–type water flow sensing device instead of a manual reset–type low water limit control.	The low water level limit control should cause fuel cutoff to the burner before the water level in the boiler falls below the lowest permissible water level established by the boiler manufacturer. A tube- or coil-type water boiler requiring forced water circulation that employs an automatic reset–type water flow sensing device instead of a manual reset–type low water level limit control should prevent burner operation when the water flow rate is inadequate to protect the boiler against overheating. The automatic reset–type water flow sensing device should also shut down the burner and prevent restarting until an adequate water flow rate is established.	UL 726, *Standard for Oil-Fired Boiler Assemblies* ASME CSD-1, *Controls and Safety Devices for Automatically Fired Boilers*
		As permitted by the authority having jurisdiction, a low water level limit control or water flow sensing device is not required to be furnished on a water boiler that has a main flame hourly input of not more than 2.85 gal/hr (10.8 L/hr).		UL 726, *Standard for Oil-Fired Boiler Assemblies*
		A low water level limit control or water flow sensing device is not required to be furnished on a water boiler installed in residences as defined by the authority having jurisdiction.		ASME CSD-1, *Controls and Safety Devices for Automatically Fired Boilers*

Table A.10.5.4 *Continued*

Appliance Type	Characteristic of Appliance to Protect	Limit Control Required		Standard References(s)
		Limit Control Description	General Operational Characteristics of Limit Control	
Boil water, *continued*	High water temperature	One manual reset–type limit control, which requires local manual intervention to reset.	When adjusted to its maximum setting allowed by a fixed stop, the limit control should limit the water temperature to not more than the maximum rated operating temperature of the boiler. For a low pressure water boiler, the maximum rated operating temperature should not exceed 250°F (121°C).	UL 726, *Standard for Oil-Fired Boiler Assemblies* ASME CSD-1, *Controls and Safety Devices for Automatically Fired Boilers*
		For a water boiler installed in a residence as defined by the authority having jurisdiction, the high temperature limit control does not need to have local manual intervention to reset and can instead have automatic reset.		ASME CSD-1, *Controls and Safety Devices for Automatically Fired Boilers*
Water heater	High water temperature	One automatic reset–type temperature regulating control, and one automatic reset–type or manual reset–type limit control.	When adjusted to its maximum setting allowed by a fixed stop, the temperature-regulating control should limit the outlet water temperature to not more than 194°F (90°C). The temperature-regulating control is permitted to limit the water temperature to not more than 200°F (93°C) if the temperature-regulating control and the limit control have cutout temperature tolerances not greater than ±5.0°F (±2.8°C). When adjusted to its maximum setting allowed by a fixed stop, the limit control should limit the outlet water temperature to not more than 210°F (99°C).	ANSI/UL 732, *Standard for Oil-Fired Storage Tank Water Heaters*

Table A.10.5.4 *Continued*

Appliance Type	Characteristic of Appliance to Protect	Limit Control Required		Standard References(s)
		Limit Control Description	General Operational Characteristics of Limit Control	
Furnace, central	Outlet air temperature	One automatic reset–type limit control. An additional auxiliary limit control, if provided, can be of the manual reset type.	When adjusted to its maximum setting allowed by a fixed stop, the limit control should prevent a central furnace from delivering air at a temperature in excess of the following: (1) 200°F (93°C) for a downflow or horizontal furnace intended for installation at the clearances specified in Form I or Form II as applicable in Table 10.6.1 (2) 250°F (121°C) for a downflow or horizontal furnace intended for installation at the clearances specified under Form III in Table 10.6.1 (3) 250°F (121°C) for a forced-air upflow furnace intended for installation at the clearances specified in Table 10.6.1 (4) 200°F (93°C) for any furnace intended for installation at less than the clearances specified in Table 10.6.1 (5) 200°F (93°C) for any furnace intended for closet or alcove installation at less than the clearances specified in Table 10.6.1	ANSI/UL 296A, *Standard for Waste Oil-Burning Air-Heating Appliances* UL 727, *Standard for Oil-Fired Central Furnaces*
Furnace, floor	Outlet air temperature	An automatic reset–type limit control. An additional auxiliary limit control, if provided, can be of the manual reset type.	When adjusted to its maximum setting allowed by a fixed stop, the limit control should prevent a floor furnace from delivering air at a temperature in excess of 250°F (121°C).	ANSI/UL 729, *Standard for Oil-Fired Floor Furnaces*
Furnace, wall	Outlet air temperature	An automatic reset or manual reset–type limit control.	When adjusted to its maximum setting allowed by a fixed stop, the limit control should prevent a wall furnace from delivering air at a temperature in excess of 250°F (121°C).	ANSI/UL 730, *Standard for Oil-Fired Wall Furnaces*

Table A.10.5.4 *Continued*

| Appliance Type | Characteristic of Appliance to Protect | Limit Control Required | | Standard References(s) |
		Limit Control Description	General Operational Characteristics of Limit Control	
Heater, air	Outlet air temperature	An automatic reset or manual reset–type limit control.	When adjusted to its maximum setting allowed by a fixed stop, the limit control should prevent an air heater from delivering air at a temperature in excess of 250°F (121°C).	UL 733, *Standard for Oil-Fired Air Heaters and Direct-Fired Heaters*
Heater, direct-fired	Outlet air temperature	An automatic reset or manual reset–type limit control.	When adjusted to its maximum setting allowed by a fixed stop, the limit control should prevent a direct-fired heater from delivering air at a temperature in excess of its designed outlet air temperature when tested as described in UL 733 and as marked on the direct-fired heater.	UL 733, *Standard for Oil-Fired Air Heaters and Direct-Fired Heaters*
Heater, kerosene-fired portable or kerosene-fired room		By inherent design and as determined by product testing. An automatic reset or manual reset–type limit control can be provided.	By inherent design and as determined by product testing.	UL 647, *Standard for Unvented Kerosene-Fired Room Heaters and Portable Heaters*
Heater, oil-fired room		By inherent design and as determined by product testing. An automatic reset or manual reset–type limit control can be provided.	By inherent design and as determined by product testing.	ANSI/UL 896, *Standard for Oil-Burning Stoves*
Heater, unit	Outlet air temperature	One automatic reset–type limit control. An additional auxiliary limit control, if provided, can be of the manual reset type.	When adjusted to its maximum setting allowed by a fixed stop, the limit control should prevent a unit heater from delivering air at a temperature in excess of the following temperatures: (1) 200°F (93°C) for a suspended-type heater with a horizontal outlet in the bottom (2) 250°F (121°C) for all other styles of unit heaters	UL 296A, *Standard for Waste Oil-Burning Air-Heating Appliances* ANSI/UL 731, *Standard for Oil-Fired Unit Heaters*

*A miniature boiler is a boiler that does not exceed any of the following limits:

(1) Maximum working gauge pressure — 100 psi (689.5 kPa)

(2) Maximum inside diameter of shell — 16 in. (406.4 mm)

(3) Maximum heating surface — 20 ft^2 (1.86 m^2)

(4) Gross volume, exclusive of casing and insulation, 5 ft^3 (0.142 m^3). The gross volume is considered to be the volume of a rectangular or cylindrical enclosure into which all the pressure parts of the boiler in their final assembled positions could be fitted. The gross volume includes gas passages that are integral with the assembled pressure parts. Projecting nozzles or fittings need not be considered in this volume.

A.10.5.5 The purpose of this requirement is to avoid interposing other controls in the limit control circuit, the failure of which can cause an unsafe condition that the limit control is intended to prevent.

A.10.6.3.1 Exception No. 2 allows a permissible variation for placing the hollow masonry to accommodate a downflow furnace, as shown in Figure 10.6.3.1.

A.11.2 The safety of installation and use of appliances of this kind depends largely on the care of the installer and the care of the user in following manufacturers' operating and installation instructions.

A.11.3.1 See UL 647, *Standard for Unvented Kerosene-Fired Room Heaters and Portable Heaters,* for specific information.

A.12.4.2 ANSI/UL 296A, *Standard for Waste Oil-Burning Air Heating Appliances,* requires the burner to be factory installed on or provided with each appliance. The evaluation of products listed under ANSI/UL 296A includes the suitability of the combination of the used-oil burner with the used oil–burning appliance and their operational characteristics relative to the construction of the combustion chamber of the appliance.

A.12.13(2) Since used oil can vary considerably in chemical and physical properties, its calorific value cannot be standardized. The conversion of 500,000 Btu/hr to 3.6 gal/hr is an approximation based on typical ASTM D 396, No. 2 fuel oil having a calorific value of approximately 140,000 Btu/gal.

Annex B Acceptable Tank Installations (Reserved)

Annex C Typical Chimney and Vent Terminations

This annex is not a part of the requirements of this NFPA document unless specifically adopted by the jurisdiction.

C.1 The diagrams in Figure C.1 illustrate typical chimney and vent terminations.

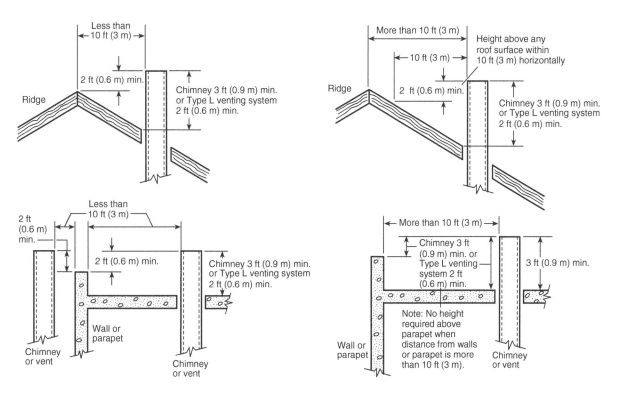

Termination more than 10 ft (3 m) from ridge, wall, or parapet

Termination less than 10 ft (3 m) from ridge, wall, or parapet

FIGURE C.1 Termination of Chimneys and Vents for Residential-Type and Low-Heat-Type Appliances.

Annex D Considerations for Combustion Equipment Firing Alternative (Nonpetroleum) Fuels

This annex is not a part of the requirements of this NFPA document unless specifically adopted by the jurisdiction.

D.1 Scope.

D.1.1 The considerations in this annex cover combustion heating appliances, such as burners and boilers, that are intended for firing alternative (nonpetroleum) fuels as a main fuel source.

D.1.2 These devices are intended for use only in commercial and industrial occupancies.

D.2 Definitions. For the purpose of this annex, terms are to be interpreted in accordance with the definitions in D.2.1 and D.2.2.

D.2.1 Alternative (Nonpetroleum) Fuel. A flammable liquid that is not covered or defined as an ASTM D 396 fuel oil, an ASTM diesel fuel, or Type K-1 kerosene.

D.2.2 Methanol. An alternative (nonpetroleum) fuel commonly identified as wood alcohol, having vapor-air mixtures that can be ignitible.

D.3 Qualifications.

D.3.1 Installation. The heating appliance should be suitable for installation in accordance with *NFPA 70, National Electrical Code,* and this standard.

D.3.2 Standard Compliance. An appliance and the burner of the appliance intended for firing an alternative (nonpetroleum) fuel should comply with the applicable requirements of ANSI/UL 296, *Standard for Oil Burners,* UL 296B, *Outline of Investigation for Combustion Equipment Firing Liquid Methanol as a Main Fuel,* UL 726, *Standard for Oil-Fired Boiler Assemblies,* and UL 795, *Standard for Commercial Industrial Gas-Heating Equipment.*

D.4 Installation and Operation Instructions.

D.4.1 The installation and operation instructions furnished with the heating equipment should include a statement to the effect that the heating appliance should be installed by a qualified installer; that is, one who is engaged in, responsible for, or thoroughly familiar with the installation and operation of commercial-industrial gas and/or oil-fired appliances, who is experienced in such work, who is familiar with the precautions required, and who will comply with all the requirements of the authority having jurisdiction for the installation.

D.4.2 If the heating equipment allows for provisions to change from an alternative (nonpetroleum) fuel source to a nonalternative fuel source, a description of the method for fuel changeover should be included in the installation and operation instructions.

D.5 Construction.

D.5.1 General. Changeover from an alternative fuel source to a nonalternative fuel source should be accomplished without manual adjustment of the heating equipment unless such adjustment is interlocked to provide safety shutdown of the heating equipment should misadjustment occur.

D.5.2 Components.

D.5.2.1 Fuel-handling components should comply with appropriate nationally recognized standards for the fuel-handling component.

D.5.2.2 Fuel-handling components should be suitable for the intended application with respect to the type of alternative fuel being handled and the exposed temperatures and pressures subjected to in service.

D.5.2.3 Internal parts of fuel-handling components (i.e., seal rings, gaskets, and the like) contacted or wetted by the fuel should be suitable for the intended applications with respect to the type of alternative fuel in contact with the part and the exposed temperatures and pressures the part(s) is subjected to in service.

D.5.2.4 Consideration should be given to long-term evaluations on internal parts of fuel-handling components (e.g, seal rings, gaskets) that are contacted or wetted by the fuel with respect to volume change and weight loss.

D.5.3 Corrosion Resistance.

D.5.3.1 Parts of the heat equipment that are in contact with combustion by-products should be resistant to corrosion from water and water vapor formed by the combustion process of the alternative fuel.

D.5.3.2 Consideration should be given to long-term evaluation of surfaces in contact with combustion by-products with respect to the effects of water and water vapor formed during the combustion process of the alternative fuel. These surfaces include, but are not limited to, the following:

(1) Combustion chamber
(2) Combustion chamber liner
(3) Heat exchanger
(4) Venting system

D.6 Performance.

D.6.1 Heating equipment should be capable of operation when firing each type of alternative and nonalternative fuel for which the equipment is rated as marked on the nameplate.

D.6.2 When the heating equipment is for operation with blends of alternative and nonalternative fuels, consideration should be given to evaluating burner operation with each blend ratio.

Annex E Relining Masonry Chimneys

This annex is not a part of the requirements of this NFPA document unless specifically adopted by the jurisdiction.

E.1 General.

E.1.1 A tile-lined masonry chimney serving an oil-fired appliance should comply with applicable building codes such as NFPA 211, *Standard for Chimneys, Fireplaces, Vents, and Solid Fuel–Burning Appliances.*

E.1.2 An additional listed metal chimney liner could be needed to reduce transient low draft during startup and acid/water condensation during cyclic operation. This is particularly true for high-mass masonry chimneys serving oil-fired appliances producing relatively low flue-gas temperature.

E.1.3 For masonry chimneys, local experience can indicate how well the construction has withstood the lower temperatures produced by a modern oil-fired appliance.

E.1.4 Evidence of potential or existing chimney damage should be determined by visual examination of the chimney and liner. Exterior indicators such as missing or loose mortar/bricks, white deposits (efflorescence) on brickwork, a leaning chimney, or water stains on interior building walls should be investigated further. Interior chimney examination with a mirror (or video camera) can reveal damaged or missing liner material.

E.1.5 The detailed characteristics of a properly constructed masonry chimney, on which to base the inspection, are included in NFPA 211, *Standard for Chimneys, Fireplaces, Vents, and Solid Fuel–Burning Appliances.* The liner must be continuous, be properly aligned and intact, and extend beyond the top of the chimney. The chimney also should have a clean-out at the base. Any debris collected in the chimney base, drop-leg, or connector should be removed and examined for content and source of debris.

E.1.6 If any doubt exists regarding the condition of the chimney, examination by an experienced professional is strongly recommended and any problems must be corrected.

E.2 Installation or Upgrade of Appliance.

E.2.1 The physical condition and suitability of an existing chimney must be checked before the installation of a new oil-fired appliance or the upgrade (new burner or reduced firing rate) of an existing appliance. The chimney should be inspected and, if needed, cleaned.

E.2.2 The current practice in existing residential oil-fired appliances is to reduce the firing rate, often to levels of 1 gal/hr (3.8 L/hr) or less, for energy conservation purposes.

E.2.3 Older oil-fired appliances are being replaced with new models having efficiencies significantly higher than 80 percent. The resulting reduction in flue gas temperatures will increase the potential for water and acid condensation in the inventory of masonry chimneys serving these appliances.

E.3 New Oil-Fired Appliances.

E.3.1 Residential-sized heating appliances sold in the United States are now required to be tested in accordance with the Annual Fuel Utilization Efficiency (AFUE) Test Procedure. This procedure is based on ASHRAE 103, *Method of Testing for Annual Fuel Utilization Efficiency of Residential Central Furnaces and Boilers.* In 1987, the National Appliance Energy Conservation Act (NAECA) was passed into federal law by Congress. This law required that, starting on January 1, 1992, for inputs less than 300,000 Btu/hr (87.9 kW), all boilers and furnaces must have an AFUE of at least 80 percent and 78 percent, respectively. Many available oil-fired boilers and furnaces already exceeded these minimum requirements, with AFUE values of 82 percent to 86 percent.

E.3.2 Modern heating appliances meeting these new requirements are being installed as replacements for older systems as well as in new construction. In the replacement of existing older systems, the venting system, largely masonry chimneys, might be oversized and in poor repair.

E.3.3 The operational flue gas temperatures for modern mid- and high-efficiency systems range from about 300°F (149°C) up to about 500°F (260°C) at the outlet of the unit. These low flue gas temperatures can be further reduced before reaching the chimney because of heat loss from the connector or through dilution when a draft regulator is used. In either case, the resulting available flue gas temperatures are frequently either insufficient to sustain adequate draft in an older, oversized masonry chimney or permit condensate to form on cold connector and chimney liner walls.

E.4 Past-Installation Inspection. After installation of a new oil-fired appliance or upgrade, if no chimney modifications were required at the time of installation, the condition of the chimney should be rechecked after 3 months and after 6 months of normal heating appliance operation to verify that the chimney is still in good condition and suitable for continued use. If any doubt exists regarding the condition of the chimney, examination by an experienced professional is again highly recommended and any problems must be corrected.

E.5 Modeling of Flue Gas Vent Systems.

E.5.1 Results of a computational analysis by Strasser and Krajewski using the Oil Heat Vent Analysis Program, OHVAP — Version 3.1 [1] to analyze a series of masonry chimney venting systems indicates that current applications of modern oil-fired heating appliances might present some difficulties with regard to formation of acid/water condensation in the chimney during winter operation.

E.5.2 OHVAP is a transient simulation program written specifically for oil-fired equipment. It uses algorithms that model flue gas composition, system pressure, draft control dilution [2, 3], system gas flow, and heat transfer in the vent system. The base case used is an exterior residential clay tile-lined masonry chimney that complies with NFPA 211, *Standard for Chimneys, Fireplaces, Vents, and Solid Fuel–Burning Appliances.*

E.5.3 For interpretation of the results from OHVAP 3.1, certain rules were applied. The minimum acceptable liner temperature was held at 95°F (35°C) during the fourth cycle and the end of the burner "on" period. The pressure at the appliance exit was held to be always negative, and the minimum acceptable draft was assumed to be 0.03 in. (7.5 Pa) of water.

E.5.4 The results of the analysis have been translated into recommended fuel firing rates, in gallons per hour, for remediating troublesome masonry chimney vent systems. The results are shown in Table E.5.4(a) through Table E.5.4(e). These tables yield recommended sizes for listed metal liners used to retrofit clay tile-lined masonry chimneys for various combinations of fuel firing rates in gallons per hour and are recommended for use when field inspection of the chimney indicates relining is necessary. Comparable tables for a listed cast-in-place liner system are shown in Table E.9.2(a) through Table E.9.2(e).

Table E.5.4(a) Listed Metal Liner Steady-State Efficiency = 88% [12% CO_2, 300°F (149°C) gross]

Height Ft	Lateral Ft	Liner 6 in.	Liner 5 in.	Liner 4 in.
10	4	0.5–1.0	0.4–0.65	0.25
	10	0.4–0.75	NR	NR
15	4	0.65–1.25	0.4–0.75	0.4
	10	0.5–1.0	0.4–0.75	0.4
20	4	0.65–1.5	0.5–0.85	0.4
	10	0.65–1.25	0.65–0.85	0.4–0.5
25	4	0.75–1.5	0.65–1.0	0.5
	10	0.85–1.25	0.65–0.85	0.5
35	4	1.0–1.75	0.75–1.0	0.5
	10	1.0–1.5	0.75–1.0	0.5
45	4	1.25–1.75	0.85–1.0	0.65
	10	1.25–1.75	0.85–1.0	0.65

For SI units, 1 ft = 0.3 m, 1 gal/hr = 3.8 L/hr.
NR: Not recommended.

Table E.5.4(b) Listed Metal Liner Steady-State Efficiency = 86% [12% CO_2, 370°F (188°C) gross]

Height Ft	Lateral Ft	Liner 6 in.	Liner 5 in.	Liner 4 in.
10	4	0.4–1.25	0.4–0.85	0.25–0.5
	10	0.4–1.25	0.4–0.75	0.25
15	4	0.5–1.5	0.4–1.0	0.4–0.5
	10	0.5–1.25	0.4–0.85	0.4–0.5
20	4	0.65–1.75	0.5–1.0	0.4–0.5
	10	0.65–1.5	0.5–1.0	0.4–0.5
25	4	0.75–1.75	0.5–1.0	0.4–0.5
	10	0.75–1.75	0.65–1.0	0.4–0.5
35	4	0.85–2.0	0.65–1.25	0.5–0.65
	10	0.85–2.0	0.65–1.25	0.5–0.65
45	4	1.0–2.25	0.75–1.25	0.65–0.75
	10	1.0–2.0	0.85–1.25	0.65–0.75

For SI units, 1 ft = 0.3 m, 1 gal/hr = 3.8 L/hr.

Table E.5.4(d) Listed Metal Liner Steady-State Efficiency = 82% [12% CO_2, 505°F (263°C) gross]

Height Ft	Lateral Ft	Liner 6 in.	Liner 5 in.	Liner 4 in.
10	4	0.4–1.5	0.25–1.0	0.25–0.5
	10	0.4–1.5	0.25–0.85	0.25–0.5
15	4	0.4–1.75	0.4–1.25	0.25–0.65
	10	0.4–1.75	0.4–1.0	0.25–0.65
20	4	0.5–2.0	0.4–1.25	0.4–0.75
	10	0.5–2.0	0.4–1.25	0.4–0.75
25	4	0.5–2.25	0.5–1.5	0.4–0.75
	10	0.65–2.0	0.5–1.25	0.4–0.75
35	4	0.65–2.25	0.65–1.5	0.5–0.85
	10	0.75–2.25	0.65–1.5	0.5–0.85
45	4	0.75–2.25	0.75–1.5	0.5–0.85
	10	0.85–2.25	0.75–1.5	0.5–0.85

For SI units, 1 ft = 0.3 m, 1 gal/hr = 3.8 L/hr.

Table E.5.4(c) Listed Metal Liner Steady-State Efficiency = 84% [12% CO_2, 440°F (227°C) gross]

Height Ft	Lateral Ft	Liner 6 in.	Liner 5 in.	Liner 4 in.
10	4	0.4–1.5	0.25–0.85	0.25–0.5
	10	0.4–1.25	0.25–0.85	0.25–0.4
15	4	0.5–1.75	0.4–1.0	0.25–0.65
	10	0.65–1.5	0.4–1.0	0.4–0.5
20	4	0.65–1.75	0.5–1.25	0.4–0.65
	10	0.65–1.75	0.5–1.0	0.4–0.5
25	4	0.65–2.0	0.5–1.25	0.4–0.75
	10	0.65–2.0	0.5–1.25	0.4–0.65
35	4	0.85–2.25	0.65–1.5	0.5–0.75
	10	0.85–2.25	0.65–1.25	0.5–0.75
45	4	1.0–2.25	0.75–1.5	0.65–0.75
	10	1.0–2.25	0.75–1.5	0.65–0.75

For SI units, 1 ft = 0.3 m, 1 gal/hr = 3.8 L/hr.

Table E.5.4(e) Listed Metal Liner Steady-State Efficiency = 80% [12% CO_2, 575°F (302°C) gross]

Height Ft	Lateral Ft	Liner 6 in.	Liner 5 in.	Liner 4 in.
10	4	0.25–1.75	0.25–1.0	0.25–0.65
	10	0.4–1.5	0.25–1.0	0.25–0.65
15	4	0.4–2.0	0.4–1.25	0.25–0.75
	10	0.5–2.0	0.4–1.25	0.25–0.75
20	4	0.4–2.25	0.4–1.5	0.4–0.85
	10	0.4–2.0	0.4–1.25	0.4–0.75
25	4	0.4–2.25	0.4–1.5	0.4–0.85
	10	0.65–2.25	0.5–1.5	0.4–0.85
35	4	0.5–2.25	0.5–1.75	0.4–0.85
	10	0.65–2.25	0.65–1.5	0.4–0.85
45	4	0.65–2.25	0.65–1.75	0.5–1.5
	10	0.65–2.25	0.65–1.75	0.5–0.85

For SI units, 1 ft = 0.3 m, 1 gal/hr = 3.8 L/hr.

E.5.5 The diameter of the metal liner should be based on the total input rating (nameplate capacity) of the appliances connected to the chimney, not the nozzle size or actual firing rate.

E.5.6 Each existing table covers a specific steady-state efficiency, chimney heights of 10 ft (3 m), 15 ft (4.5 m), 20 ft (6 m), 25 ft (7.5 m), 35 ft (10.5 m), and 45 ft (13.5 m), with lateral distances of 4 ft (1.2 m) and 10 ft (3 m) for each chimney height. After selecting the proper table and the proper row in that table, the appropriate range of firing rates for each liner size is easily found through interpolation. *(See Sections E.8 and E.10 for examples of the use and application of these tables.)*

E.6 Condensation. The issue of water condensation in masonry chimneys has been documented, as have been the issues

of damage to masonry, mortar, and liners in chimneys often due to improper construction [4, 5]. However, quantitative correlation between condensation rates and changes in chimney life has not been determined.

E.7 Evaluation of Results.

E.7.1 In interpreting the OHVAP simulation results to develop the recommendations, two criteria for successful system performance are applied during the fourth cycle at the end of the appliance burner "on" period. These criteria are as follows:

(1) A minimum available winter-time [42°F (5.6°C) outside ambient temperature] pressure at the appliance of about −0.03 in. of water column (−7.5 Pascals) and a negative pressure at all times at the appliance during burner "on"

(2) A minimum chimney liner surface temperature at the top of the chimney at the end of the burner "on" period of about 95°F (35°C) (water dew point of diluted flue gas)

E.7.2 The tables are derived (by simulation) on the basis of 12 percent CO_2, but the recommendations are valid for CO_2 levels between 10 percent and 14 percent. A single right-hand elbow is included in the connector between the appliance and the chimney. In addition, a simple air gap is assumed to surround a smooth metal liner within the chimney, as described in Section E.5. Any additional elbows in the connector or dislocations (offsets from vertical) in the chimney might require limitations of the upper firing rate.

E.7.3 In common practice, a flexible liner might be used, which is rougher than the liner used in the analysis. In this application, to meet chimney capacity requirements, a reduction of about 15 percent in firing rate is in order.

E.8 Examples of Use of the Chimney Venting Tables. The relined exterior chimney venting tables, Table E.5.4(a) through Table E.5.4(e), are included in this annex. In order to use the tables, the user should first determine the approximate steady-state efficiency of the appliance being vented. This approximation can be made using one of three methods for a specific appliance:

(1) Flue loss method
(2) Heating capacity method
(3) AFUE method

E.8.1 The Flue Loss Method involves the adjustment of the appliance burner for a satisfactory maximum flue gas CO_2 level (minimum excess combustion air) and a trace to No. 1 smoke (Bacharach scale) after a minimum of 10 minutes of operation. The flue gas temperature is then measured at the appliance exit, and the value is used to select the table or tables for use in obtaining the recommended vent size and firing rate. If the measured temperature falls between two tables, the recommendations contained in the tables above and below that of the measured temperature should be interpolated. When all measurements are completed, the appliance burner adjustments should be checked and readjusted if needed to conform with CO_2 and smoke level settings as indicated in the equipment manufacturers' specifications.

E.8.2 The Heating Capacity Method involves dividing the appliance heating capacity (usually given in thousands of Btu per hour) by the input rate (converted to thousands of Btu per hour) multiplied by 100. This result will provide an approximate steady-state efficiency value for selecting the table or tables used in interpolating the recommended vent size and firing rate.

E.8.3 The AFUE Method involves the determination of the AFUE for the appliance at hand. The AFUE for a particular model of the appliance can be obtained from annual listings published by the Gas Appliances Manufacturers' Association or promotional material provided by the appliance manufacturer. An estimate of the steady-state efficiency can be obtained by adding 1 percentage point to the AFUE value of a hydronic boiler and 2 percentage points to the AFUE value of a warm air furnace. This steady-state efficiency value can then be used in selecting the table or tables used in interpolating the recommended vent size and firing rate.

E.8.4 The following three working examples illustrate the required procedures for evaluating the recommendations offered in the tables given in Section E.5.

E.8.4.1 The first example assumes that an appliance firing 1 gal/hr (3.8 L/hr) has an efficiency determined by the AFUE method to be 88 percent (AFUE = 87 percent + 1 percent = 88 percent). The total length of the connector is 7 ft (2.1 m), and the chimney is 20 ft (6 m) high. From Table E.5.4(a), it is determined that the chimney is listed, but the connector length is not; therefore, the user should interpolate between the table entries for connectors of 4 ft (1.2 m) and 10 ft (3 m) long. Looking in the 4 ft (1.2 m) connector row, it can be seen that only a 6 in. (150 mm) liner will suffice, 5 in. (125 mm) being rated only for lower firing rates of 0.5 gal/hr to 0.85 gal/hr and 4 in. (100 mm) being rated only for a lower firing rate of 0.4 gal/hr (1.5 L/hr). In the 10 ft (3 m) connector row, again, the 6 in. (150 mm) liner will do. In this case the size selection can only be a 6 in. (150 mm) liner.

E.8.4.2 The second example assumes that applying the Flue Loss Method resulted in a measured flue gas temperature of 523°F (273°C) after burner adjustment. The firing rate for the appliance is 1 gal/hr (3.8 L/hr). In addition, the total straight connector length is 7 ft (2.1 m) into a 22 ft (6.6 m) chimney. Note that some of the parameters of the system are not precisely located among the tables. The method to be employed here is to bracket the system parameters and interpolate an appropriate recommendation. Using a connector/chimney combination of 4/20 at 505°F (263°C) and 575°F (302°C) at 1 gal/hr (3.8 L/hr), the recommendations allow for a 4 in. (100 mm), 5 in. (125 mm), or 6 in. (150 mm) diameter metal liner. Similarly, for a connector/chimney combination of 10/25 at 505°F (263°C) and 575°F (302°C) at 1 gal/hr (3.8 L/hr), the same three liner sizes are allowed. In this instance, the choice is clear in that any of the three metal liner sizes would be satisfactory. If the firing rate had been 1.5 gal/hr (5.7 L/hr), however, the metal liner size would have been restricted to 6 in. (150 mm) due to the high end limit of 1.25 gal/hr (4.8 L/hr) defined under the connector/chimney size of 10/25 at 505°F (263°C). On the other hand, if the firing rate had been 0.5 gal/hr (1.9 L/hr), the metal liner choices would have no restrictions due to the low end limit of 0.4 gal/hr (1.5 L/hr) defined under the same connector/chimney combination and flue gas temperature.

E.8.4.3 The third example assumes that applying the Heating Capacity Method resulted in an estimated steady-state efficiency of 87 percent with a firing rate of 0.85 gal/hr (3.2 L/hr). This case also assumes that a 4 ft (1.2 m) connector is used between the appliance and the chimney, which stands 25 ft (7.5 m) above the breech. In the table for a steady-state efficiency of 88 percent, the 5 in. (125 mm) and 6 in. (150 mm) metal liners are shown as satisfactory. In the table for a steady-state efficiency of 86 percent, the 5 in. (125 mm) and 6 in. (150 mm) metal liners are also satisfactory. Based on average values for firing rates between the two tables, the 5 in. (125 mm) and 6 in. (150 mm) liners should be satisfactory for a steady-state efficiency of 87 percent. In any case, an adjustment of firing rate, an increase of draft, or an increase in the excess combustion air would help serve to bring the system out of any marginal performance condition.

E.9 Analysis of Relined Chimneys.

E.9.1 A series of relined masonry chimney venting systems was analyzed using OHVAP 3.1. This case was modeled as an exterior residential chimney using a listed cast-in-place system, which is used to replace an 8 in. (20 cm) square clay tile lining. The cast-in-place system meets the requirements of NFPA 211, *Standard for Chimneys, Fireplaces, Vents, and Solid Fuel–Burning Appliances.* For this analysis, the minimum acceptable liner temperature was held to 75°F (24°C) during the burner "on" period of the fourth cycle. This minimum temperature exceeds the predicted minimum liner temperature in as-found residential masonry chimneys. The pressure at the appliance exit was held to be always negative, and the minimum acceptable draft was held to be 0.03 in. (7.5 Pa) of water.

E.9.2 These results have been translated into recommended fuel-firing rates, in gallons per hour, for remediating troublesome masonry chimney vent systems. The results are shown in Table E.9.2(a) through Table E.9.2(e). These tables yield recommended sizes for listed cast-in-place lining systems used to retrofit clay tile–lined masonry chimneys for various combinations of fuel–firing rates and are recommended for use when field inspection of the chimney indicates relining is necessary.

Table E.9.2(a) Listed Cast-in-Place Liner Steady-State Efficiency = 88% [12% CO_2, 300°F (149°C) gross]

Height Ft	Lateral Ft	Liner 6 in.	Liner 5 in.	Liner 4 in.
10	4	0.5–1.0	0.4–0.5	NR
	10	0.5–0.85	NR	NR
15	4	0.65–1.5	0.5–1.0	0.4–0.5
	10	0.75–1.25	0.75–0.85	NR
20	4	0.75–1.5	0.65–1.0	0.5
	10	0.75–1.5	0.65–0.85	NR
25	4	0.85–1.75	0.75–1.0	NR
	10	0.85–1.5	0.75–0.85	NR
35	4	1.25–1.75	1.0	NR
	10	1.25–1.5	NR	NR
45	4	1.5–1.75	NR	NR
	10	1.5	NR	NR

For SI units, 1 ft = 0.3 m, 1 gal/hr = 3.8 L/hr.
NR: Not recommended.

Table E.9.2(b) Listed Cast-in-Place Liner Steady-State Efficiency = 86% [12% CO_2, 370°F (188°C) gross]

Height Ft	Lateral Ft	Liner 6 in.	Liner 5 in.	Liner 4 in.
10	4	0.5–1.25	0.4–0.85	0.4–0.5
	10	0.5–1.25	0.4–0.65	0.4–0.5
15	4	0.65–1.75	0.5–1.0	0.4–0.65
	10	0.65–1.5	0.5–1.0	0.4–0.5
20	4	0.65–2.0	0.65–1.0	0.5–0.65
	10	0.75–1.75	0.65–0.85	0.5
25	4	0.75–2.0	0.65–1.25	0.65
	10	0.85–1.75	0.65–1.0	NR
35	4	1.0–2.0	0.85–1.25	NR
	10	1.0–2.0	0.85–1.0	NR
45	4	1.25–2.0	1.0	NR
	10	1.25–1.75	1.0	NR

For SI units, 1 ft = 0.3 m, 1 gal/hr = 3.8 L/hr.
NR: Not recommended.

E.9.3 Each table covers a specific steady-state efficiency, chimney heights of 10 ft (3 m), 15 ft (4.5 m), 20 ft (6 m), 25 ft (7.5 m), 35 ft (10.5 m), and 45 ft (13.5 m) and lateral distances of 4 ft (1.2 m) and 10 ft (3 m) for each chimney height. After selecting the proper table and the proper row in that table, the appropriate range of firing rates for each liner size is easily found.

E.10 Example.

E.10.1 This example assumes that applying the Flue Loss Method resulted in a measured flue gas temperature of 485°F (252°C) after burner adjustment. The firing rate for the appliance is 1.1 gal/hr (4.2 L/hr). In addition, the total straight connector length is 5 ft (1.5 m) into an 18 ft (5.5 m) chimney. Note that some of the parameters of the system are not pre-

Table E.9.2(c) Listed Cast-in-Place Liner Steady-State Efficiency = 84% [12% CO_2, 440°F (227°C) gross]

Height Ft	Lateral Ft	Liner 6 in.	Liner 5 in.	Liner 4 in.
10	4	0.4–1.5	0.4–1.0	0.25–0.5
	10	0.5–1.25	0.4–0.85	0.4–0.5
15	4	0.5–2.0	0.4–1.25	0.4–0.65
	10	0.65–1.75	0.5–1.0	0.4–0.65
20	4	0.65–2.0	0.5–1.25	0.4–0.75
	10	0.65–2.0	0.5–1.25	0.5–0.65
25	4	0.75–2.25	0.65–1.25	0.5–0.75
	10	0.75–2.0	0.65–1.0	0.65
35	4	0.85–2.25	0.75–1.25	0.65
	10	1.0–2.25	0.75–1.25	NR
45	4	1.25–2.25	1.0–1.25	NR
	10	1.25–2.25	1.0–1.25	NR

For SI units, 1 ft = 0.3 m, 1 gal/hr = 3.8 L/hr.
NR: Not recommended.

Table E.9.2(d) Listed Cast-in-Place Liner Steady-State Efficiency = 82% [12% CO_2, 505°F (263°C) gross]

Height Ft	Lateral Ft	Liner 6 in.	Liner 5 in.	Liner 4 in.
10	4	0.4–1.5	0.4–1.0	0.25–0.65
	10	0.4–1.5	0.4–1.0	0.25–0.65
15	4	0.5–2.0	0.4–1.25	0.4–0.75
	10	0.5–2.0	0.4–1.25	0.4–0.65
20	4	0.65–2.0	0.5–1.5	0.4–0.75
	10	0.65–2.0	0.5–1.25	0.4–0.75
25	4	0.65–2.25	0.65–1.5	0.5–0.75
	10	0.65–2.25	0.65–1.25	0.5–0.75
35	4	0.85–2.25	0.65–1.5	0.65–0.75
	10	0.85–2.25	0.75–1.25	0.65
45	4	1.0–2.25	0.85–1.5	0.75
	10	1.0–2.25	0.85–1.25	NR

For SI units, 1 ft = 0.3 m, 1 gal/hr = 3.8 L/hr.
NR: Not recommended.

Table E.9.2(e) Listed Cast-in-Place Liner Steady-State Efficiency = 80% [12% CO_2, 575°F (302°C) gross]

Height Ft	Lateral Ft	Liner 6 in.	Liner 5 in.	Liner 4 in.
10	4	0.4–1.75	0.25–1.0	0.25–0.65
	10	0.5–1.5	0.4–1.0	0.25–0.5
15	4	0.5–2.25	0.4–1.25	0.4–0.85
	10	0.4–2.0	0.4–1.25	0.4–0.75
20	4	0.5–2.25	0.4–1.5	0.4–0.85
	10	0.65–2.25	0.5–1.25	0.4–0.75
25	4	0.65–2.25	0.5–1.5	0.4–0.85
	10	0.65–2.25	0.5–1.5	0.5–0.75
35	4	0.75–2.25	0.65–1.5	0.65–0.85
	10	0.75–2.25	0.65–1.5	0.65–0.75
45	4	0.85–2.25	0.75–1.5	0.75–0.85
	10	1.0–2.25	0.85–1.5	0.75

For SI units, 1 ft = 0.3 m, 1 gal/hr = 3.8 L/hr.
NR: Not recommended.

cisely located in these tables. This refers to Table E.9.2(c) and Table E.9.2(d).

E.10.2 The method to be employed here is to bracket the system parameters and interpolate to secure an appropriate option. Using the connector/chimney combinations of 4/15 and 4/20 at 440°F (227°C) and 505°F (263°C) at 1.1 gal/hr (4.2 L/hr), the recommendations allow for a 5 in. (125 mm) or 6 in. (150 mm) diameter liner system. Similarly, for connector/chimney combinations of 10/15 and 10/20 at 440°F (227°C) and 505°F (263°C) at 1.1 gal/hr (4.2 L/hr), the same two liner systems are allowed. In this instance, the choice is clear: any of the two liner systems would be satisfactory.

E.10.3 If the firing rate had been 1.5 gal/hr (5.7 L/hr), however, the liner system might be marginal for the 5 in. (125 mm) size. The choice would have been restricted to the 6 in. (150 mm) size, due to the high end limit of 1.25 gal/hr (4.7 L/hr) defined under connector/chimney size combinations of 4/20 and 10/20 at 440°F (227°C). On the other hand, if the firing rate had been 0.5 gal/hr (1.9 L/hr), the liner system choices might be marginal for the 6 in. (150 mm) size. Thus, following the above logic, the recommendation would have been restricted to the 4 in. (100 mm) and 5 in. (125 mm) sizes, due to the low end limit of 0.65 gal/hr (2.5 L/hr) specified under the same connector/chimney combinations and flue gas temperatures given above.

E.11 Situations Where Simple Relining Is Not Recommended. In some cases, the relining system performance does not meet the minimum appliance draft or the minimum liner temperature criteria, regardless of treatment. These are shown as "NR," meaning they are not recommended for simple relined chimney venting. In these cases, an improvement in system performance can be achieved by using a listed alternative venting system. These alternatives include, but are not limited to, the following: listed power vents, where draft is not sufficient, or listed factory-built metal chimneys, where liner wall temperatures are too low.

E.12 Warm Weather Firing Rates.

E.12.1 The maximum warm outdoor weather capacity in terms of firing rate (gallons per hour) for a masonry chimney constructed according to NFPA 211, *Standard for Chimneys, Fireplaces, Vents, and Solid Fuel–Burning Appliances,* is a function of chimney height and the steady-state efficiency of the attached appliance. The warm outdoor weather ambient temperature [76°F (24°C)] used in this analysis was based on the July average for 10 major U.S. cities, taken from Chapter 30, Table 3, of the *ASHRAE Handbook of Fundamentals* [6].

E.12.2 The predicted performance of these chimneys was analyzed using OHVAP 3.1. The predicted maximum firing rates were selected assuming the pressure within the chimney system remained below 0.03 in. (7.5 Pa) of water and positive for no more than 10 seconds at burner start. Table E.12.2 shows this maximum capacity for a masonry chimney consisting of one row of outer brick, an air gap, and an 8 in. × 8 in. (200 mm × 200 mm) square flue liner.

Table E.12.2 Warm Weather Firing Rate for Masonry Chimneys in Gallons per Hour

Appliance Efficiency, Steady State	Chimney Height Above Connector					
	10 ft (3 m)	15 ft (4.6 m)	20 ft (6 m)	25 ft (7.6 m)	35 ft (10.7 m)	45 ft (13.7 m)
80%	2.0	2.25	2.25	2.25	2.25	2.25
82%	2.0	2.25	2.25	2.25	2.25	2.25
84%	1.75	2.0	2.25	2.25	2.25	2.25
86%	1.25	1.5	1.75	2.0	2.25	2.25
88%	NR	1.0	1.0	1.25	1.75	2.0

NR: Not recommended.

E.13 References. [1] Strasser, J., et al., "Oil-Heat Vent Analysis Program" (OHVAP), *Users Manual Engineering Report — Informal Report BNL-63668,* Brookhaven National Laboratories, Upton, NY, 1994.

[2] Krajewski, R. F., "Development of Oil Heat Venting Tables," Oil Heat Technology Conference and Workshop, No. 94-15, 1994.

[3] Butcher, T., et al., "Chimney Related Energy Losses in Oil-Fired Heating Systems: Configuration Effects and Venting Alternatives," BNL-46021, 1990.

[4] Gorden, E., et al., "Masonry Chimney Inspection and Relining," AGAL Unpublished Topical Report, 1990.

[5] Kam, V. P., et al., "Masonry Chimneys and Liners," AGAL Draft Topical Report, 1991.

[6] *ASHRAE Handbook of Fundamentals,* American Society of Heating, Refrigeration, and Air Conditioning Engineers, 1997.

Annex F Informational References

F.1 Referenced Publications. The documents or portions thereof listed in this annex are referenced within the informational sections of this standard and are not part of the requirements of this document unless also listed in Chapter 2 for other reasons.

F.1.1 NFPA Publications. National Fire Protection Association, 1 Batterymarch Park, Quincy, MA 02169-7471.

NFPA 30, *Flammable and Combustible Liquids Code*, 2008 edition.

NFPA 30A, *Code for Motor Fuel Dispensing Facilities and Repair Garages*, 2008 edition.

NFPA 70®, National Electrical Code®, 2011 edition.

NFPA 211, *Standard for Chimneys, Fireplaces, Vents, and Solid Fuel–Burning Appliances*, 2010 edition.

F.1.2 Other Publications.

F.1.2.1 API Publications. American Petroleum Institute, 1220 L Street, NW, Washington, DC 20005-4070.

API Standard 650, *Specifications for Welded Steel Tanks for Oil Storage.*

F.1.2.2 ASHRAE Publications. American Society of Heating, Refrigerating and Air Conditioning Engineers, Inc., 1791 Tullie Circle, NE, Atlanta, GA 30329-2305.

ASHRAE 103, *Method of Testing for Annual Fuel Utilization Efficiency of Residential Central Furnaces and Boilers*, 1993.

ASHRAE *Handbook of Fundamentals*, 1997.

F.1.2.3 ASME Publications. American Society of Mechanical Engineers, Three Park Avenue, New York, NY 10016-5990.

ASME CSD-1, *Controls and Safety Devices for Automatically Fired Boilers*, 1995.

F.1.2.4 ASTM Publications. ASTM International, 100 Barr Harbor Drive, P.O. Box C700, West Conshohocken, PA 19428-2959.

ASTM D 396, *Standard Specification for Fuel Oils*, 1990.

F.1.2.5 PEI Publications. Petroleum Equipment Institute, P.O. Box 2380, Tulsa, OK 74101-2380.

RP-100, *Recommended Practices for Installation of Underground Liquid Storage Systems*, 1990.

F.1.2.6 STI/SPFA Publications. Steel Tank Institute/Steel Plate Fabricators Association, 944 Donata Court, Lake Zurich, IL 60047.

STI ACT-100, *Specification for External Corrosion Protection of FRP Composite Steel Underground Tanks, F894*, 2010.

F.1.2.7 UL Publications. Underwriters Laboratories Inc., 333 Pfingsten Road, Northbrook, IL 60062-2096.

ANSI/UL 296, *Standard for Oil Burners*, 2003, with revisions through January 2009.

ANSI/UL 296A, *Standard for Waste Oil-Burning Air Heating Appliances*, 1995.

UL 296B, *Outline of Investigation for Combustion Equipment Firing Liquid Methanol as a Main Fuel*, 2006.

UL 647, *Standard for Unvented Kerosene-Fired Room Heaters and Portable Heaters*, 1993.

UL 726, *Standard for Oil-Fired Boiler Assemblies*, 1995.

UL 727, *Standard for Oil-Fired Central Furnaces*, 2006.

ANSI/UL 729, *Standard for Oil-Fired Floor Furnaces*, 2003.

ANSI/UL 730, *Standard for Oil-Fired Wall Furnaces*, 2003.

ANSI/UL 731, *Standard for Oil-Fired Unit Heaters*, 1995.

ANSI/UL 732, *Standard for Oil-Fired Storage Tank Water Heaters*, 1995.

UL 733, *Standard for Oil-Fired Air Heaters and Direct-Fired Heaters*, 1993.

UL 795, *Standard for Commercial Industrial Gas-Heating Equipment*, 2006.

ANSI/UL 896, *Standard for Oil-Burning Stoves*, 1993.

UL 1316, *Standard for Glass-Fiber-Reinforced Plastic Underground Storage Tanks for Petroleum Products, Alcohols, and Alcohol-Gasoline Mixtures*, 1994.

UL 1746, *Standard for External Corrosion Protection Systems for Steel Underground Storage Tanks*, 2007.

F.2 Informational References. The following documents or portions thereof are listed here as informational resources only. They are not a part of the requirements of this document.

Butcher, T., et al., "Chimney Related Energy Losses in Oil-Fired Heating Systems: Configuration Effects and Venting Alternatives," BNL-46021, 1990.

Gorden, E., et al., "Masonry Chimney Inspection and Relining," AGAL Unpublished Topical Report, 1990.

Kam, V. P., et al., "Masonry Chimneys and Liners," AGAL Draft Topical Report, 1991.

Krajewski, R. F., "Development of Oil Heat Venting Tables," Oil Heat Technology Conference and Workshop, No. 94-15, 1994.

Strasser, J., et al., "Oil-Heat Vent Analysis Program" (OH-VAP), *Users Manual Engineering Report — Informal Report BNL-63668*, Brookhaven National Laboratories, Upton, NY, 1994.

F.3 References for Extracts in Informational Sections. (Reserved)

Index

Copyright © 2010 National Fire Protection Association. All Rights Reserved.

Sequence of Events for the Standards Development Process

Once the current edition is published, a Standard is opened for Public Input.

Step 1 – Input Stage

- Input accepted from the public or other committees for consideration to develop the First Draft
- Technical Committee holds First Draft Meeting to revise Standard (23 weeks); Technical Committee(s) with Correlating Committee (10 weeks)
- Technical Committee ballots on First Draft (12 weeks); Technical Committee(s) with Correlating Committee (11 weeks)
- Correlating Committee First Draft Meeting (9 weeks)
- Correlating Committee ballots on First Draft (5 weeks)
- First Draft Report posted on the document information page

Step 2 – Comment Stage

- Public Comments accepted on First Draft (10 weeks) following posting of First Draft Report
- If Standard does not receive Public Comments and the Technical Committee chooses not to hold a Second Draft meeting, the Standard becomes a Consent Standard and is sent directly to the Standards Council for issuance (see Step 4) or
- Technical Committee holds Second Draft Meeting (21 weeks); Technical Committee(s) with Correlating Committee (7 weeks)
- Technical Committee ballots on Second Draft (11 weeks); Technical Committee(s) with Correlating Committee (10 weeks)
- Correlating Committee Second Draft Meeting (9 weeks)
- Correlating Committee ballots on Second Draft (8 weeks)
- Second Draft Report posted on the document information page

Step 3 – NFPA Technical Meeting

- Notice of Intent to Make a Motion (NITMAM) accepted (5 weeks) following the posting of Second Draft Report
- NITMAMs are reviewed and valid motions are certified by the Motions Committee for presentation at the NFPA Technical Meeting
- NFPA membership meets each June at the NFPA Technical Meeting to act on Standards with "Certified Amending Motions" (certified NITMAMs)
- Committee(s) vote on any successful amendments to the Technical Committee Reports made by the NFPA membership at the NFPA Technical Meeting

Step 4 – Council Appeals and Issuance of Standard

- Notification of intent to file an appeal to the Standards Council on Technical Meeting action must be filed within 20 days of the NFPA Technical Meeting
- Standards Council decides, based on all evidence, whether to issue the standard or to take other action

Notes:

1. Time periods are approximate; refer to published schedules for actual dates.
2. Annual revision cycle documents with certified amending motions take approximately 101 weeks to complete.
3. Fall revision cycle documents receiving certified amending motions take approximately 141 weeks to complete.

Committee Membership Classifications[1,2,3,4]

The following classifications apply to Committee members and represent their principal interest in the activity of the Committee.

1. M   *Manufacturer:* A representative of a maker or marketer of a product, assembly, or system, or portion thereof, that is affected by the standard.
2. U   *User:* A representative of an entity that is subject to the provisions of the standard or that voluntarily uses the standard.
3. IM   *Installer/Maintainer:* A representative of an entity that is in the business of installing or maintaining a product, assembly, or system affected by the standard.
4. L   *Labor:* A labor representative or employee concerned with safety in the workplace.
5. RT   *Applied Research/Testing Laboratory:* A representative of an independent testing laboratory or independent applied research organization that promulgates and/or enforces standards.
6. E   *Enforcing Authority:* A representative of an agency or an organization that promulgates and/or enforces standards.
7. I   *Insurance:* A representative of an insurance company, broker, agent, bureau, or inspection agency.
8. C   *Consumer:* A person who is or represents the ultimate purchaser of a product, system, or service affected by the standard, but who is not included in (2).
9. SE   *Special Expert:* A person not representing (1) through (8) and who has special expertise in the scope of the standard or portion thereof.

NOTE 1: "Standard" connotes code, standard, recommended practice, or guide.

NOTE 2: A representative includes an employee.

NOTE 3: While these classifications will be used by the Standards Council to achieve a balance for Technical Committees, the Standards Council may determine that new classifications of member or unique interests need representation in order to foster the best possible Committee deliberations on any project. In this connection, the Standards Council may make such appointments as it deems appropriate in the public interest, such as the classification of "Utilities" in the National Electrical Code Committee.

NOTE 4: Representatives of subsidiaries of any group are generally considered to have the same classification as the parent organization.

Submitting Public Input / Public Comment Through the Online Submission System

Soon after the current edition is published, a Standard is open for Public Input.

Before accessing the Online Submission System, you must first sign in at www.nfpa.org. *Note: You will be asked to sign-in or create a free online account with NFPA before using this system:*

a. Click on Sign In at the upper right side of the page.
b. Under the Codes and Standards heading, click on the "List of NFPA Codes & Standards," and then select your document from the list or use one of the search features.

OR

a. Go directly to your specific document information page by typing the convenient shortcut link of www.nfpa.org/document# (Example: NFPA 921 would be www.nfpa.org/921). Sign in at the upper right side of the page.

To begin your Public Input, select the link "The next edition of this standard is now open for Public Input" located on the About tab, Current & Prior Editions tab, and the Next Edition tab. Alternatively, the Next Edition tab includes a link to Submit Public Input online.

At this point, the NFPA Standards Development Site will open showing details for the document you have selected. This "Document Home" page site includes an explanatory introduction, information on the current document phase and closing date, a left-hand navigation panel that includes useful links, a document Table of Contents, and icons at the top you can click for Help when using the site. The Help icons and navigation panel will be visible except when you are actually in the process of creating a Public Input.

Once the First Draft Report becomes available there is a Public Comment period during which anyone may submit a Public Comment on the First Draft. Any objections or further related changes to the content of the First Draft must be submitted at the Comment stage.

To submit a Public Comment you may access the online submission system utilizing the same steps as previously explained for the submission of Public Input.

For further information on submitting public input and public comments, go to: http://www.nfpa.org/publicinput.

Other Resources Available on the Document Information Pages

About tab: View general document and subject-related information.

Current & Prior Editions tab: Research current and previous edition information on a Standard.

Next Edition tab: Follow the committee's progress in the processing of a Standard in its next revision cycle.

Technical Committee tab: View current committee member rosters or apply to a committee.

Technical Questions tab: For members and Public Sector Officials/AHJs to submit questions about codes and standards to NFPA staff. Our Technical Questions Service provides a convenient way to receive timely and consistent technical assistance when you need to know more about NFPA codes and standards relevant to your work. Responses are provided by NFPA staff on an informal basis.

Products & Training tab: List of NFPA's publications and training available for purchase.

Information on the NFPA Standards Development Process

I. Applicable Regulations. The primary rules governing the processing of NFPA standards (codes, standards, recommended practices, and guides) are the NFPA *Regulations Governing the Development of NFPA Standards (Regs)*. Other applicable rules include NFPA *Bylaws*, NFPA *Technical Meeting Convention Rules*, NFPA *Guide for the Conduct of Participants in the NFPA Standards Development Process*, and the NFPA *Regulations Governing Petitions to the Board of Directors from Decisions of the Standards Council*. Most of these rules and regulations are contained in the *NFPA Standards Directory*. For copies of the *Directory*, contact Codes and Standards Administration at NFPA Headquarters; all these documents are also available on the NFPA website at "www.nfpa.org."

The following is general information on the NFPA process. All participants, however, should refer to the actual rules and regulations for a full understanding of this process and for the criteria that govern participation.

II. Technical Committee Report. The Technical Committee Report is defined as "the Report of the responsible Committee(s), in accordance with the Regulations, in preparation of a new or revised NFPA Standard." The Technical Committee Report is in two parts and consists of the First Draft Report and the Second Draft Report. (See *Regs* at Section 1.4.)

III. Step 1: First Draft Report. The First Draft Report is defined as "Part one of the Technical Committee Report, which documents the Input Stage." The First Draft Report consists of the First Draft, Public Input, Committee Input, Committee and Correlating Committee Statements, Correlating Notes, and Ballot Statements. (See *Regs* at 4.2.5.2 and Section 4.3.) Any objection to an action in the First Draft Report must be raised through the filing of an appropriate Comment for consideration in the Second Draft Report or the objection will be considered resolved. [See *Regs* at 4.3.1(b).]

IV. Step 2: Second Draft Report. The Second Draft Report is defined as "Part two of the Technical Committee Report, which documents the Comment Stage." The Second Draft Report consists of the Second Draft, Public Comments with corresponding Committee Actions and Committee Statements, Correlating Notes and their respective Committee Statements, Committee Comments, Correlating Revisions, and Ballot Statements. (See *Regs* at 4.2.5.2 and Section 4.4.) The First Draft Report and the Second Draft Report together constitute the Technical Committee Report. Any outstanding objection following the Second Draft Report must be raised through an appropriate Amending Motion at the NFPA Technical Meeting or the objection will be considered resolved. [See *Regs* at 4.4.1(b).]

V. Step 3a: Action at NFPA Technical Meeting. Following the publication of the Second Draft Report, there is a period during which those wishing to make proper Amending Motions on the Technical Committee Reports must signal their intention by submitting a Notice of Intent to Make a Motion (NITMAM). (See *Regs* at 4.5.2.) Standards that receive notice of proper Amending Motions (Certified Amending Motions) will be presented for action at the annual June NFPA Technical Meeting. At the meeting, the NFPA membership can consider and act on these Certified Amending Motions as well as Follow-up Amending Motions, that is, motions that become necessary as a result of a previous successful Amending Motion. (See 4.5.3.2 through 4.5.3.6 and Table 1, Columns 1-3 of *Regs* for a summary of the available Amending Motions and who may make them.) Any outstanding objection following action at an NFPA Technical Meeting (and any further Technical Committee consideration following successful Amending Motions, see *Regs* at 4.5.3.7 through 4.6.5.3) must be raised through an appeal to the Standards Council or it will be considered to be resolved.

VI. Step 3b: Documents Forwarded Directly to the Council. Where no NITMAM is received and certified in accordance with the Technical Meeting Convention Rules, the standard is forwarded directly to the Standards Council for action on issuance. Objections are deemed to be resolved for these documents. (See *Regs* at 4.5.2.5.)

VII. Step 4a: Council Appeals. Anyone can appeal to the Standards Council concerning procedural or substantive matters related to the development, content, or issuance of any document of the NFPA or on matters within the purview of the authority of the Council, as established by the Bylaws and as determined by the Board of Directors. Such appeals must be in written form and filed with the Secretary of the Standards Council (see *Regs* at Section 1.6). Time constraints for filing an appeal must be in accordance with 1.6.2 of the *Regs*. Objections are deemed to be resolved if not pursued at this level.

VIII. Step 4b: Document Issuance. The Standards Council is the issuer of all documents (see Article 8 of *Bylaws*). The Council acts on the issuance of a document presented for action at an NFPA Technical Meeting within 75 days from the date of the recommendation from the NFPA Technical Meeting, unless this period is extended by the Council (see *Regs* at 4.7.2). For documents forwarded directly to the Standards Council, the Council acts on the issuance of the document at its next scheduled meeting, or at such other meeting as the Council may determine (see *Regs* at 4.5.2.5 and 4.7.4).

IX. Petitions to the Board of Directors. The Standards Council has been delegated the responsibility for the administration of the codes and standards development process and the issuance of documents. However, where extraordinary circumstances requiring the intervention of the Board of Directors exist, the Board of Directors may take any action necessary to fulfill its obligations to preserve the integrity of the codes and standards development process and to protect the interests of the NFPA. The rules for petitioning the Board of Directors can be found in the *Regulations Governing Petitions to the Board of Directors from Decisions of the Standards Council* and in Section 1.7 of the *Regs*.

X. For More Information. The program for the NFPA Technical Meeting (as well as the NFPA website as information becomes available) should be consulted for the date on which each report scheduled for consideration at the meeting will be presented. To view the First Draft Report and Second Draft Report as well as information on NFPA rules and for up-to-date information on schedules and deadlines for processing NFPA documents, check the NFPA website (www.nfpa.org/docinfo) or contact NFPA Codes & Standards Administration at (617) 984-7246.